10

THE ESSENTIAL RULES FOR BEATING THE MARKET

10

THE ESSENTIAL RULES FOR BEATING THE MARKET

Michael Turner

WILEY

John Wiley & Sons, Inc.

Published by John Wiley & Sons, Inc., Hoboken, New Jersey.
Published simultaneously in Canada.

For general information on our other products and services or for technical
support, please contact our Customer Care Department within the United States at
(800) 762-2974, outside the United States at (317) 572-3993 or fax (317) 572-4002.

Wiley also publishes its books in a variety of electronic formats. Some content that
appears in print may not be available in electronic books. For more information
about Wiley products, visit our web site at www.wiley.com.

Library of Congress Cataloging-in-Publication Data:
Turner, Michael K., 1947-
    10 : the essential rules for beating the market / Michael K. Turner.
        p.   cm.
    Includes index.
    ISBN 978-0-470-29261-7 (cloth)
        1. Investments.   2. Speculation.   I. Title.   II. Title: Ten, the essential rules
    for beating the market.
    HG4521.T87   2009
    332.6—dc22
                                                                    2008036132

Printed in the United States of America

10 9 8 7 6 5 4 3 2 1

*For Sue, Amy, Bryan, Will, Christie, and
my grandchildren. I couldn't have done
any of it without you!*

Contents

Foreword   ix

Preface   xi

Acknowledgments   xix

Introduction   1

Rule 1   Think like a Fundamentalist   15

Rule 2   Spend Your Money Wisely—The Value Rule   37

Rule 3   Trade like a Technician   53

Rule 4   The Stop Loss Rule   71

Rule 5   Never Marry a Stock (For Adults Only!)   93

Rule 6   Follow Only "Some" Insider Trading   103

Rule 7   Watch the Institutional Ownership   109

Rule 8   Stay Diversified   121

Rule 9   Balance Your Risk through Smart
Asset Allocation   147

Rule 10   Make a Lot More Money by
Timing the Market   155

Epilogue Making the Commitment to Being a
Rules-Based Investor   173

Appendix A Understanding Stop Loss Orders   175

Appendix B Scoring the Fundamentals   179

About the Author   **187**

Index   **189**

Foreword

Many of you may know me from your own investing track record. Perhaps we have met at some of the trading show venues. The first time I met Mike Turner I was impressed by his skills to make the market work for him, rather than the other way around. We both enjoy the excitement of investing in the stock market. I was delighted to hear that Mike was writing a book about his 10 essential rules for beating the market. Being an engineer, Mike's approach to investing is very structured. I was afraid his writing might come across as overly analytical. But, after reading his book, I was amazed at how Mike is able to convey his very successful investment techniques and methodologies into a fun to read and yet powerful book that will make you a much better stock market investor.

I have spent my life building portfolios and teaching thousands of investors how to improve their success rate in the stock market. There have been thousands of books written on the subject. But Mike's 10 rules are truly a "best practices" how-to book for every investor. You will not want to put this book down once you start reading it.

The market, of late, has been extremely tough on everyone. But Mike's own portfolio, which explicitly follows his rules, not only came through this tough market unscathed, but generated returns that most investors only dream of. He accomplished this amazing feat due to following the rules he conceived to help him navigate these rough waters. We are fortunate that he has chosen to share them with all of us who wish to capture the best the market has to offer, regardless of what it throws at us from time to time! Being in the market doesn't have to be intimidating, and it doesn't have to produce sleepless nights. We simply need a plan to follow. If you put Mike's 10 rules to work, you will have an unbeatable investment plan.

This book is a must read for both serious and novice investors. His no-nonsense style, mixed with commonsense rules, can immensely help investors make better and wiser decisions. If he had asked me what to title the book, I would have said, "The 10 Commandments for Investing," for it represents rules by which all investors should live their investing lives.

Of Mike's 10 rules, it would be hard for me to pick a favorite one, since they all represent good commonsense rules for investors to follow. If I were forced to pick a favorite, however, it would be Rule 1: "Think Like a Fundamentalist." As I've learned over recent years, fundamental investing has increasingly gone out of fashion with Wall Street, which seems more obsessed with "structured management" (i.e., building better benchmarks), and "arbitrage strategies" (i.e., quantitative long/short models). These two concepts often represent up to half the trading volume on many days and have given rise to increasing stock market volatility, as we have witnessed, all of which makes traders very nervous. If individual investors would make their trading decision based on fundamentals, then the stocks they select typically would be much less volatile, and would move in a more orderly and predictable manner. This would be extremely beneficial to holding onto gains and preventing large losses.

But what I like most about Mike's approach to building a disciplined investment strategy is that he combines the very best of a fundamental approach but relies heavily on technical trends to pick the best time to buy and sell.

I really like his approach to selling. I agree with him that most investors have no idea when to sell. His straightforward approach of turning that unknown into a simple but profound formula is pure genius. There should be more engineers running investment firms. We would have far fewer financial catastrophes if there were more strategic and disciplined investors who would use Mike's 10 rules for investing!

Each of us wishes to make the best of the market—in good times and especially in bad. In this regard I feel that Mike is a visionary and will provide you with a set of rules to guide you on a steady course so you do not get distracted or derailed completely by the stock market's gyrations. I know you will enjoy Mike's book and come to use it as a reference tool every time you are evaluating new stocks to buy or sell.

I hope you will put Mike's rules to work for yourself and see that you, too, can make consistent profits in the stock market.

Thank you, Mike, for generously sharing these rules with all of us in the trading world.

LOUIS NAVELLIER

Preface

Odds are you do not know me, and, as such, it seems appropriate that I tell you a little about who I am and how it is that I have written this book. After all, I am going to ask you to make the 10 rules in this book an integral part of your life when it comes to investing in and profiting by investing in the stock market.

You should know that I do not come from the world of finance. In fact, when I started out in my professional career, I never dreamed that I would be where I am today. I'll get to that part in a bit.

You see, I started out in life as a civil engineer. My goal was to build massive structures that would be of great benefit to mankind. But a fledgling engineer just graduating from college is never put in charge of building great structures. In fact, most new civil engineering grads are lucky if they get to design handrails for second-story apartments—but, I digress.

This preface is not an autobiography. I would not insult your intelligence by any such self-aggrandizement. However, it is important for you to know how someone like myself, who never intended to have a career in finance, much less become a professional portfolio and hedge fund manager, has managed to come to the point where you would care to take the time to learn how to become a master stock investor by reading my thoughts and ideas and how I approach making money in the stock market.

The reason why this story should matter to you is that, in a lot of ways, I suspect that you and I are very much alike. You are probably not a finance professional. You probably have a day job or are retired from one. You do, however, have a very strong desire to take control of your own investments and make wise, profit-generating stock market decisions. You want to make significant returns through your stock investments and you don't want to take a lot of risk.

I am of the same mind. . . .

I also want you to believe that you can make money in the stock market and become more competitive with your returns than a lot of the so-called investment or fund managers. Regardless of your background, you can, with the help of this book, learn how to generate consistent profits in the stock market.

Here is why I know this to be true. My story:

My early (very early) professional life was all about being an engineer. My first job was assistant city engineer for Edmond, Oklahoma. There, I met a wonderful man by the name of Augie Gale. Augie was many years my senior, and we rapidly became good friends. One day, over lunch, he handed me a book and said I should read it. He said it was the greatest book he had ever read on the stock market. He was enthusiastic and made it sound like it was almost impossible to lose money in the stock market if a person would just do what the author suggested.

Intrigued, I took the book home and read it through. It was a numerical analysis approach to knowing when to buy and when to sell stocks. It was one of the earliest books on technical analysis, but in 1973, that term wasn't nearly so common as it is today.

I was fascinated by the concept and especially the mathematical approach taken by the author. Being in my first job out of college, I didn't have any money to invest in the market, but I was sure—even then—that one day I would take the concept of statistically analyzing stocks to make buy/sell decisions. At least, that became a dream of mine. One reason why I was so intrigued by the algorithms in the book was that I knew it was going to take a computer program to do what the author was doing by hand. Software engineering was really my first love when I was in college and it was a significant component of my formal education.

I wanted my own copy of the book, so I tried to find a copy at the local bookstores. This was long before online bookstores or the Internet. No one carried the book, but I was able to find the address of the author and wrote to him to see if he would sell me a copy. He not only sold me a copy, but began sending me periodic updates to his book as he refined his algorithms and strategies. I corresponded with the author for several years.

Each time I got an update to the book in the mail, I immediately read it through to see what nuance had been added and pored over every new rule and/or rule modification.

I began writing pseudo code and flowcharts on the steps and processes. I would dream about how to get the data constructed and how I would need to have a mainframe computer just to process the rules and data and generate the charts. I know, this all sounds very geeky—and, it was. But that's what we engineers do. We like huge problems that require a methodical set of logical steps that build one upon another until a final solution can be generated. Building large, complex software designs is very akin to building large, complex structures. The big difference is that one set of structures is very physical and made of concrete and steel; the other is equally (if not more so) complex but is made up of bits and bytes.

I kept my designs and algorithms in notebooks that I would often dig out and review and rethink, but, in the meantime, I had to put food on the table. As most careers evolve, mine evolved along the lines of engineering and construction, at least for a few years.

I went on to become a materials engineer for a nuclear power plant, and then I founded and ran a commercial and residential construction company. In 1980, just about the time that some of the very first small computers came on the market, I was given the opportunity to start a software design and development company. I was finally able to get into my first real love: computer programming.

For the next 17 years, my software applications company developed enterprise-level software systems for the preclinical drug safety industry. By the time I sold the company in 1997, we had most of the major pharmaceutical companies in the world as clients and a majority of the world's medical research universities were using our software.

After selling the company in 1997, I had a fairly nice nest egg of cash. I wasn't sure what I wanted to do next, but I knew I needed to put that nest egg to work. So I did what I thought was the smart thing to do: I put my money with one of the biggest investment firms on Wall Street and assumed that I would see my nest egg grow at least 8 to 10 percent per year. Based on this firm's record, I was actually hoping to see a much higher return.

I can remember those first few quarterly reports. Each one would show that I had less money in my account than the previous quarter. I still recall the knot I would get in the pit of my stomach when I would open my quarterly report. I couldn't believe that I was reading the reports correctly. So I went in to see my account manager.

The ability of this firm to obfuscate performance (or, in this case, the lack of performance) was amazing. But, after digging through all the charts and tables and graphs that showed I was doing exceptionally well when comparing my performance to a bunch of indexes I had never heard of, I would leave thinking that I must be overreacting to the fact that my nest egg was getting smaller each quarter—a *lot* smaller.

The next quarter, I went in to speak with my account manager again. And again I listened to him tell me how wonderful my investments were doing and the great job he was doing by moving me from bonds to stocks and back to bonds and then back to mutual funds. I should feel very privileged to have my money with some of the greatest fund managers in the world. He would go on and on about how these fund managers were beating this or that index. I was fortunate to have such a talented and thoughtful account manager. He was doing a masterful job. During my visits, he would have several computer screens all buzzing with account information and stock and market information. He was very impressive. At the end of the discussion, I would leave thinking I just hadn't given my account manager enough time to really generate the returns he was capable of. He would tell me of the huge amount of money he had under advisement and would impress me with the names of some of his clients.

All the while, my nest egg was getting smaller and smaller.

Keep in mind that this was the 1997–1999 time frame. You could throw a dart at a wall of stocks and make money in those days.

Finally, it got to a point where I couldn't bear to even open the quarterly reports. It was during this time that I pulled out my design notes and my old, dog-eared, massively highlighted book on technical analysis. I decided that I would write some programs and see if I could get my system to pick some stocks and time the buy and the sell action.

I did, and I immediately began to see promise in the algorithms.

I went to a few investor conferences and began seriously considering taking over my own stock market investing. I don't mind telling you that I approached that decision with more than a fair amount of trepidation. After all, who did I think I was? How could I possibly compete with the investment giants of Wall Street?

But, after two long, agonizing years of seeing my nest egg almost cut in half, I finally decided that the worst I could do was probably better than a 45 percent loss. So I walked into that big, fancy investment firm and fired my account manager and moved the money into my own self-managed account at a discount brokerage firm.

If I was going to take responsibility for my family's financial future, I knew that I needed to know more than just what was in that technical analysis book that had followed me around for nearly 30 years.

I began doing a *lot* of research and a *lot* of reading. I researched many, many investment methodologies. I looked at every technical approach from Fibonacci analysis to Elliot Wave theory to neural networks. One conclusion that I arrived at was that if any of these technical methodologies always worked, everyone would use that method. But there was no consensus approach (and there still isn't) to the best technical analysis.[1]

My research (and, thankfully, a bit of common sense) also led me down the path of fundamental analysis. The gurus of fundamental analysis almost universally discounted the value of technical analysis. These fundamental masters believe in an efficient market theory, and as such, put no stock whatsoever in a technical approach to timing the market or repeatable pricing trends.

Efficient Market Hypothesis (EMH)

Asserts that the market prices of equities (e.g., stocks, bonds, or property) already reflect all known information. The EMH states that it is impossible to consistently outperform the market by using any information that the market already knows, except through luck. Information or news in the EMH is defined as anything that may affect prices that is unknowable in the present and thus appears randomly in the future.

I found it amazing that these two camps were at odds with each other, when it seems intuitively obvious (in an engineer's mind) that these two camps should embrace each other's input and methodology. It rapidly became clear to me that I needed a system that did both a fundamental and a technical analysis of stocks such that I would not only know what to buy (fundamental analysis), but would know when to buy and when to sell (technical analysis).

---

[1]Based on the premise that all relevant information is already reflected by prices, technical analysts believe it is redundant to do fundamental analysis.

I then assumed that someone surely, by this time, had developed a sophisticated stock analysis tool that the average investor could use to manage his/her stock investments. So, I went to a number of investor conferences, did a lot of research on the Internet, and tried out several systems—all to no avail. None of them had the right combination of technical and fundamental analysis rules.

I knew I had to develop my own system using my own methodology. So, in 1999, I began the design and development effort.

A task that I thought might take a year or so actually took closer to three years. But, after several thousand man-hours of design and development and decades of back-testing, my software tool was ready to be put to use.

I remember some of my first trades as if it were yesterday. It is one thing to do fictitious trades; it is quite another to put real money (my nest egg, or what was left of it) into the market using a system that I believed in, but had never trusted my financial future to. It was an auspicious and stressful step off the edge of financial security.

But I rapidly began to see my nest egg grow. Even when the market began collapsing in 2000, I continued to make money. Not every trade was a winning trade, but way more trades were winners than losers. I began to see that I not only had a great methodology of combining both technical and fundamental analysis, but the software system I had designed and developed was more productive than I could have imagined.

Since my big Wall Street account manager had taken me from the realm of semiretirement to needing to build another company, I began to look at how to make this system available to other investors who were trapped into either having to let Wall Street manage their money or try to find multiple systems, tools, and methodologies to do what we had in one very powerful stock market investing system. That is when TurnerTrends, Inc. was launched in January 2002 with our first portfolio: The Market Trend portfolio.[2]

From there, we launched three more portfolios and in 2007 opened our investor tools to individual investors to use. (The portfolios are: The ETF Total Return; the 10 Essential Rules; and the Covered Call. The ETF Total Return portfolio is an ETF-only portfolio. The 10 Essential Rules portfolio is the companion portfolio to this

---

[2]This is a portfolio of 10 stocks and 10 exchange-traded funds (ETFs).

book. The Covered Call portfolio is a unique approach to using covered calls.

Then, in 2008, we launched Sabinal Capital Investments, LLC, a managed account service, and the Sabinal Capital Investments Market Bias Fund.

My point in sharing all of this with you is so you can understand that when I approached solving the problem of growing my nest egg through smart, safe investments in the stock market, I did not start out with any preconceived notions about the "right" or "wrong" way to "properly" buy and sell stocks. I approached this problem like any engineer would approach a problem. You must first identify the problem. In this case, the problem was "avoid losing money in the stock market and replace that with making consistent profits in the stock market."

Next, I identified all the inputs to the solution, which includes historical stock prices, stock fundamentals, diversification requirements, asset allocation requirements, risk mitigation requirements, and historical market trends.

I had a set of knowns (empirical data about equities and markets) and a set of unknowns (what to buy, when to buy and when to sell). Without boring you with more analogies, my job then was to take a set of equations and balance those equations, with the result being consistent profits in the stock market, while maintaining low levels of risk.

I approached this entire process from a nonbiased numerical methods perspective. I had no preconceived biases or belief structures. I was when I started—and I still am today—very agnostic when it comes to buying and selling equities. I really don't care about the companies except from a fundamental perspective. I don't really care about technical trends except from the timing of when to buy and when to sell. My methodology is very "quant" driven,[3] and it is a methodology that you can learn to use very quickly.

I have done all the hard work. You don't have to spend thousands of man-hours and several years of your life to learn the principles and rules that I have for you in this book. You can read this in a weekend and start making a lot more money when the markets open this coming Monday.

Enjoy!

---

[3]A computerized numerical analysis process.

Acknowledgments

I want to thank several people who have helped me along the way to the world of stock market trading.

First, I want to thank the professors at Oklahoma State University, where I obtained my degree in civil engineering. They instilled in me the belief that with the right set of rules and formulas, there isn't any problem that can't be solved.

The next person I want to thank is Augie Gale. If only you had whispered in my ear, "Go into the stock market, Mike," it would have not taken me so long to arrive at this wonderful place. I am grateful he ignited the spark.

To my loyal partners in this business, I want to thank you for your sound counsel. I appreciate your dedication to our purpose of helping individual investors reach their financial dreams.

Tom Meyer, where would I be today, if I hadn't met you! You were the first one to see the vision. Thank you for believing in me. Thank you for your optimism and can-do attitude!

Ira, what an iconic sage you are. Always ready to teach and forever keeping me out of trouble. I tell everyone you're the smartest trader in the world. Thank you, man!

I also want to thank my dear friends, Charlie and Kay Liles, for their remarkable efforts to read and critique the first very rough drafts (numerous times). You are wonderful people, fun to be around, and scholarly to boot! Thanks for everything!

Thanks also to Ken, my "unofficial director of quality assurance" and fellow engineer. Your help has been insightful and your encouragement has been unfailing, my friend.

Special thanks to my son, Will, who was instrumental in the design and development of the database and the programming algorithms we use every weekend to analyze over 6,000 stocks in our database. Your work on creating the web site and investor tools allows our clients to build their own world-class portfolios. You and I have enjoyed the rare privilege of working together on our common dreams. Your countless hours of hard work have been sacrificial, and I especially want to thank your loving wife, Christie, for her support for both of us. Thanks to both of you for arranging special occasions for me to be with the grandchildren.

To our daughter, Amy, thank you for searching to find those few spare moments in my life and filling them up with my grandchildren. Thank you for always encouraging, always defending, and working tirelessly whenever asked. Bryan, thank you for your unwavering support.

And to my grandchildren, who crawled on my lap while I was working and asked, "What are stocks, Pop"? Perhaps I will get the honor of teaching you someday. When I couldn't attend a particular family function, or was late to others, you understood. I am grateful for your love and affection.

Thank you to my editor, David Pugh, who saw there was more here than could be contained in a 45-minute PowerPoint presentation. Your enthusiastic push got things started, and I am immensely grateful.

Thank you to all my subscriber/friends who call and e-mail me with encouraging words. I take your thoughts to heart and appreciate them more than you know. Working for you is a joy, and I love every minute of it.

And last, but certainly not least, special thanks to my wife, Sue. Thank you for your faith, encouragement, and for allowing me to reach for my dreams. You're the best, my love.

Introduction

So you're interested in the stock market. Who can blame you? Who can possibly ignore the wonderfully dynamic, fast-paced, living, breathing world of buying and selling stocks? It has fascinated me for years. And I assume it intrigues you, too (otherwise, you would not be reading this book).

How excited would you be to consistently make profits in the stock market and to consistently beat the major indexes? What if you could double your net worth every three to four years, only spend a few (very few) hours a week doing it, and keep your downside risk extremely low? If you read this book and follow my 10 Essential Rules for consistent profits in the stock market, you will achieve this lofty goal and completely change your investing life—forever!

The key to making consistent profits in the stock market is having a well-defined set of trading rules and the discipline to follow those rules—in good markets, bad markets, up markets, down markets, or flat markets.

The stock market is an incredible marketplace, where buyers and sellers can almost instantly reach a conclusion where both are convinced that they have each made the better deal. There is an old saying that in every trade there are two geniuses and two idiots. The buyer believes the stock he's buying will move up in price and generate a profit. The seller believes the stock he holds is about to move down in price and will generate a loss. The seller wants out and the buyer wants in. The buyer believes he is the genius. The seller believes he (the seller) is the genius. They each believe the other side of the trade is the idiot. Both are thrilled with their trading prowess. Both are resolute in their convictions; and depending on their time horizon, both can be right and both can be wrong. Such is the world of trading stocks!

It is with that story in mind that I have taken on the task of writing this book. It is my hope that, after reading and studying my "10 Essential Rules for Beating the Market," you will always be the genius and never the idiot! I had a gentleman ask me not long ago what I was trying to say by writing this book and I told him I wanted it to be a "how-to" book, not a "hope-to" book, for when I ask people what their objective is for getting into the market, most of them say, "To make money, and hopefully not lose any money"!

10: The Essential Rules for Beating the Market is a book that will teach you how to make consistent profits in the stock market. You will learn when to buy and when to sell. You will learn how to diminish risk and maximize gain. You will learn that rules, not emotions, should dictate each and every trade.

Whether you are a seasoned investor with decades of experience or a novice just getting ready to jump in and make your first trade, this book is for you. Perhaps you are an investor who has made some not-so-great trades in the past and are looking for ways to help you make better trading decisions. Perhaps you are completely happy with your trading results, but are interested in learning all you can about investing in the stock market and value different approaches and opinions. Maybe you are intrigued by the fact that this book combines both a technical and a fundamental approach to investing. Maybe you have a small nest egg and you want to grow it into a huge nest egg. There could be any number of reasons why you began searching in this section of the bookstore. Regardless, you have found the right book at the right time in your investment life!

Why Invest in the Market at All?

"What are your reasons for investing in the stock market?" I'm sure you have given some thought to this question. Investors will give any one or more of the following reasons why they invest in the stock market, including:

- For their retirement.
- For their children's college education.
- To pay for a vacation home.

- To make a higher rate of return than a money market account.
- For their grandchildren's future.
- So their kids won't have to take care of them when they are old.
- To provide funds for charitable causes.
- For the excitement and fun of it.

The list can be virtually endless. But I suspect their true underlying goal in all of these reasons is to make a profit. You are, no doubt, thinking that seems intuitively obvious! However, a lot of investors do not have a well-thought-out plan as to how to accomplish that goal. If your first objective is making a profit and making it consistently when buying and selling stocks, then this is the ideal book for you. I intend to show you how to do just that!

In all cases, your first priority *should be* to make a profit. In addition to profitability being the primary, although not always stated, objective of every stock market investor, you can be sure that the second most desired objective of every investor is to have *consistent* profits and *lower* risk.

Rarely are these objectives an actual component of the average investor's investment strategy. After you read this book, they will be. You can change your investment life forever and for the better. I will teach you how to make consistent profits in the stock market. You will learn how to incorporate 10 rules I have developed into your investment methodology and you will start making more money in the stock market than you ever thought possible.

Most people I talk with desire low risks and reasonable returns on their investments. I can teach you how to improve on that desire. You will learn how to minimize risk and generate exceptional returns. I want you to set a goal to generate at least 23.8 percent per year and to keep your risks at an absolute minimum. If you achieve that goal, you will be doubling your nest egg every three years. This is not a "get-rich-quick scheme" but rather a "get-rich" formula. These rules require commitment, discipline, common sense, the absence of emotion, and a modicum of hard work. Think where you would be today if you had been able to reach that goal over the past 10 years (or in the next 10). You will not reach that goal every year. No one does, but you will reach it more times than you ever thought possible.

Why Most Investors Fail to Make Consistent Profits in the Stock Market

Before I divulge the 10 rules, I want to tell you what I have observed to be the key reasons why most investors fail to make consistent profits in the stock market. It is likely that you and I have never met. Regardless, I know something about you. For one thing, you are definitely *not* an average investor. The average investor rarely reads or studies books that might require them to change their investment strategy. They will stay in their investment comfort zone, where they continue to make the same mistakes over and over and they never achieve a level of generating consistent and significant profits in the stock market.

Since you are reading this book, you are not an average investor. But you may be making a number of the same investment mistakes that average investors make. It is important to identify these investment mistakes before you will be able to fully embrace the investment methodology and strategies contained in this book.

The very good news is that you are doing something about changing your approach to investing. You are looking for a better way to invest in the stock market or a way to incrementally improve your stock investment prowess. This separates you from the vast majority of "average" investors. You are definitely above average. By the time you finish this book, you will be far above average.

Before you learn the right way to invest in the stock market, it is important to understand why most investors fail to make consistent profits in the stock market. A lot of what is behind the cause of losing money in the stock market can be summarized in just two reasons:

1. Investors who are better at making consistent losses in the market, instead of consistent profits, generally do not have a solid set of rules that govern what to buy, when to buy, and when to sell. These investors buy stocks without a clear plan for what to do if the investment grows in value or decreases in value. They may know *why* they got in, but they have no clue on *how* and *when* to get out. These investors do not have an investment strategy or methodology.

2. The second major reason why most investors do not do well in the market is ego and emotion. It is amazing how many

investors will hang onto a stock just because they do not want to admit that the decision to buy that stock was not a good decision. These investors will do almost anything to avoid making hard decisions because of their fear of loss, the desire for gain or their refusal to admit a mistake.

I am a big believer in rules and formulas. Here are a couple of formulas to illustrate my point. I hope you will embrace them.

No Rules + Emotion = Consistent *Losses* in the Stock Market

Here's an example of what I mean:

When the market sells off or when a fundamentally strong stock suddenly drops in share price, you will often hear a big name TV personality tell you that "the market is wrong." It may come as a shock to you (and particularly the TV personality), but the market is never "wrong." It is never "right." The market is what it is. The only reason why someone would say the market is wrong is when, in fact, they are wrong. But their ego wants them to believe that they couldn't make a mistake, so everyone else must be wrong. Everyone else is "the market." When you think you are right and everyone else is wrong, it is likely that your ego has taken over from rational logic. Average investors trade a lot on emotion and ego. The key to making consistent profits in the stock market is to have an investment strategy that is based on rules, not emotion. So here is your next formula:

A Good Set of Trading Rules − Emotion = Consistent *Profits* in the Stock Market

Over most reasonable time horizons of at least a year or more, the investor who sticks to his/her rules and makes investment decisions based strictly on those rules will consistently make more money than investors who jump from one set of rules to another, or worse, jump from a decent set of rules to no rules at all.

Without a solid set of rules to follow, most investors become victims of human emotion, where they become far better at making consistent *losses* than consistent *profits*.

This doesn't mean every trade you make will be a winning trade. That never happens. You will have winning trades and losing trades. It is a fact of life and of the stock market. However, by reading and studying this book, you will learn how to make more winning trades than losing trades and how to make more money in your winning trades than you lose in your losing trades. Keep in mind, your goal is to make 23.8 percent per year. You want to double your nest egg every three years, if possible. You will reach that goal with winning trades and some losing trades. But you can and will reach that goal more often than not if you develop a strong set of smart, anticipatory rules that will serve you well in any kind of market. You will find the 10 rules in this book to be exactly those kinds of rules.

The Dream World of Mutual Funds and Indexes

The vast majority of stock market investors can only dream of making 10 percent per year; much less 15 percent, 20 percent, or even the lofty 23.8 percent. Unfortunately, the average investor rarely makes more than the rate of inflation. Each year, many millions of investors significantly underperform the market. This is true for active stock market investors who buy and sell stocks. This low rate of return is almost guaranteed for those investors who don't buy and sell stocks but, instead, put their nest egg in mutual funds.

Did you know that approximately 80 percent of all the mutual funds underperform the stock market? So, if the market has a down year or several down years, 80 percent of mutual funds will do even worse. Other than as required in some 401(k) plans, there is no reason why anyone should put money into a mutual fund.[1]

Surprisingly and unfortunately, between 1984 and 2003, the average equity investor earned a paltry 2.57 percent annually, compared to the 3.14 percent rate of inflation. This is according to DALBAR, Inc.,[2] a leading financial services market research firm. This means that the average investor actually loses money every year in terms of real dollars.

After all, if you can't make a better return than inflation, you might as well just put your money into a savings account and draw money market rates. You will still lose money due to inflation (or, at

---

[1]See "Why Mutual Funds Are a Rip-off" on www.turnertrends.com.

[2]Headquartered in Boston, with additional offices in Toronto, DALBAR develops standards for, and provides research, ratings, and rankings of intangible factors to the mutual fund, broker/dealer, discount brokerage, life insurance, and banking industries. They include investor behavior, customer satisfaction, service quality, communications, Internet services, and financial-professional ratings.

best, make a very small and virtually insignificant return), but you will have eliminated all of your risk. At least you know what your return will be, and subject to the demise of the U.S. government, your investments are reasonably safe.

Contrary to what some high-profile stock market mavens[3] claim, putting your hard-earned money into an index fund is no panacea either. For example, if you had invested in an S&P 500 index fund in January 2000, by the end of the 2006, your nest egg would have experienced an annual loss of –0.36 percent. So just blindly putting money into index funds is not the way to generate 20 percent or more per year.

My point is this: **You should not assume that you can make consistent profits in the stock market by just throwing your money into an index fund or a mutual fund. You also cannot indiscriminately buy and sell stocks without a clear plan and set of trading rules. And you certainly cannot let *emotion* control or impact your trading.**

Out of the Frying Pan and into the Fire—or How Emotions Can Ruin Your Day

The typical investor starts out with extreme caution about jumping into the market. Perhaps he/she got burned previously and doesn't want to make the same mistake twice.

The market starts booming and stock prices start rising. At first, the investor is wary that this might be a false signal that the market will soon nosedive once again. But, no, the market keeps climbing.

Then the talking heads and the investment press all start exclaiming how a certain stock (symbol: XYZ) has made a big move

---

[3]One such famous market maven is John Bogle. Bogle is famous for his insistence, in numerous media appearances and in writing, on the superiority of index funds over traditional actively managed mutual funds. He believes that it is folly to attempt to pick actively managed mutual funds and expect their performance to beat a well-run index fund over a long period of time. I agree with Bogle's assessment of mutual funds, but he is completely wrong that investing in index funds is a sure way to long-term wealth generation. Index funds work in bull markets unless you short them in bear markets. A well-balanced portfolio will have some exchange-traded funds, but I would never advise a client to just put your money in index funds and then hope they will someday be worth more money. This is nothing more than another failed attempt at justifying a buy-and-hold investment strategy.

up and it looks as if there is no end in sight. The investor wants to get in this stock but is afraid that he has waited too long.

Then, another big story hits with more good news on XYZ. It moves up again, this time even more than before. And putting more pressure on the investor is the fact that the overall market continues to move up more and more, perhaps moving into record territory.

The investor can stand it no longer! He buys in, afraid of missing out. The investor is excited about his decision. He is finally in the bull market with one of the highest flyers in the group. The fundamentals are great. He just "knows" he's made the right decision. He wishes he had gotten in earlier, but "better late than never," he always says.

Initially, XYZ continues to move up, more and more. The investor pats himself on the back and nods approvingly at his investment acumen. Just look at his investment! He is up 15 percent in just three weeks. He begins to brag to his buddies about his new stock and the fact that he is "taking advantage of this bull market." Three weeks later, he is up another 20 percent! He is a stock-picking genius!

Then disappointing news comes out about the economy, and his prize stock takes a hit. But our investor hangs on. The fundamentals haven't really changed. The bad news was more industry related than stock related. But the stock's price drops even more. His stock loses 15 percent, but he is still showing a profit. Now is not the time to give up on this great stock. The fall-off in the market is just a normal correction that always occurs in bull markets. His stock will soon recover and get back to reaching new multiyear highs again. He's not worried—after all, bull markets have to "climb a wall of worry."[4] He's not going to get out now; this pull-back won't last, he says.

The stock does not move higher. It moves lower—much lower. Now our investor is showing a paper loss of 10 percent. The investor continues to hang on. He's still not too worried. The stock's

---

[4]Some investors believe that bull markets tend to move appreciably higher in the face of economic and geopolitical uncertainties. These market-impacting uncertainties become the "wall" that the bull market has to overcome to move higher and is considered a strong indicator that differentiates a market rally from a true bull market.

fundamentals haven't changed. He made the right decision when he bought this stock. Only the "weak hands" would "fold" or sell now, he tells himself. He is not one of those wishy-washy kinds of investor. He's *much smarter* than that!

The stock drops again. The investor is now down 30 percent. Fear starts to creep into the investor's mind. He has lost so much. But he believes in the company. He talks himself into cutting his loss in half if he'll just double the number of shares that he owns. So he buys more shares. He has convinced himself that he is buying the stock "on sale." He reasons that by averaging down the cost of his shares, he has now only lost half as much. Instead of being down 30 percent, his logic tells him he is now only down 15 percent. He feels a little better.

Doubling the Number of Shares Owned

This is also known as *averaging down* or *doubling down*, which is an ego-based strategy used to reduce the average price paid per share by buying an equal number of shares at a lower price.

But the stock's price takes another hit and moves significantly lower. His loss now is more than 50 percent!

Panic sets in. He can't believe he's done this to himself—again! He doesn't know what to do. He wishes he had never bought XYZ. He can't sleep at night. He tells himself that he is cursed and should have never even thought about getting back in the market. He finally gives up. He sells. He lost over 50 percent of his investment!

The next day, the stock suddenly recovers and begins a process of reversing. He can't believe it. Its price moves higher and higher; eventually retracing all of its recent pullback.

But where is our investor now? He is no longer in the market. He swears he will never make that mistake again. For a while, he is smart enough to realize that without a solid investment strategy, he won't be able to make money in the market. He knows he doesn't have such a strategy and doesn't know how to put one together. So he ignores the market for a few months or even a few years. But, eventually, he begins to think he will just dabble a little in the market again. He has a few successes. His confidence begins to grow. It isn't long before he's a market genius again.

Once again, he starts the whole process of buying at the top, and before long he is selling at the bottom. Occasionally, our average investor will hit a home run. But, more times than not, he ends up in a never-ending cycle of buying high and selling low. It is the mantra of way too many investors. I wonder if you recognize anyone here—a friend, a family member, or yourself perhaps?

Don't feel discouraged. Even if you recognize yourself in the above story, the good news is you are going to learn how to completely and forever avoid this buy-high, sell-low cycle. Let's discuss some ways to fix this.

You *Can* Remove Emotion from Investing

So how do we go about controlling our emotions? After all, we all have them. That's what distinguishes us as humans. We may not want to admit it, but we all have emotions and attitudes that can and do impact our decisions for buying and selling stocks. These emotions can include: fear, panic, greed, arrogance, happiness, unhappiness, love, infatuation, and ego. These emotions often do an extensive amount of damage to a good investment strategy. At least with regard to investing, we would all be better served if we could remove these emotions from our psyche.

But none of us can completely shut off these emotions. They are a part of our nature. They make up our personality. However, I believe you *can* keep these emotions from adversely impacting your investment strategy. And, by doing so, you can become a smarter, wealthier investor and not be continually buffeted by emotional ups and downs. Let's study how two emotions, greed and arrogance, can influence our trading decisions.

We looked at an investor who let the fear of missing out on a bull market allow him to get in at the wrong time. We saw how greed kept him from making a profit by keeping him in a certain stock too long. We saw how fear and ego caused him to make terrible mistakes that cost him 50 percent of his investment.

When greed manifests itself, it becomes an all-consuming, propelling force. You no longer take the appropriate time to analyze your decisions. Suddenly, you find you're no longer relying on your rules. All you can think about is profit—big profits. Anything else is not satisfying.

Errors in judgment are the result of the momentum of greed. Mistakes will be made. When all you can think about is making an enormously huge fortune, then you set yourself up for failure. It is likely you are not doing a good job of following your disciplined investment strategy. Without a disciplined investment strategy, the odds dramatically increase that you will achieve consistent losses instead of consistent profits.

Now, let's look at what happens when arrogance rears its ugly head. I want to say here that it is a good thing to be happy about your portfolio's performance. But when happiness turns into arrogance, consistency in making profits becomes a thing of the past. And it is so easy to let arrogance come into your thinking. When your portfolio has several weeks of strong, consistent profits, you begin to say, "I haven't picked a bad stock yet. I'm a stock-picking genius!"

Along the way, you begin to tire of following a disciplined approach to investing. You start making small mistakes. Instead of following your rules, you start following your hunches.

Hunch trading is one of the worst ways to trade, but it is one the best ways to lose money. Maybe some of these mistakes actually make you more money. (Almost every investor, in a bull market, becomes a stock-picking genius. It's often said that in a bull market you can throw darts at the stock symbols and pick winners! Wouldn't that be fun?)

When your arrogance overwhelms your common sense, you begin to set yourself up for potentially significant losses. Why? Because you have abandoned your rules for investing and now just rely on your "intuition." Intuition is not a good investment strategy and will eventually lead to disaster. Don't let your successes cloud your judgment. Stay *humble.* Stay *smart.* Stay *disciplined!* And make up your mind to *commit* to following these 10 rules I am about to share with you.

If you agree to let a commonsense set of rules govern your trading actions to the extent that you trade only by these rules, then any emotion that might cause you to make poor investment decisions will absolutely be eliminated.

Trust me—you can do this. Once you've mastered my 10 rules, you will be amazed at how free you become from worry and second-guessing.

When you invest in the stock market, you need to do so in a calm, rational frame of mind. Allow the rules to make the decisions for you, and you will no longer be riding the roller coaster of emotion. Let the rules rule.

It's Time to Kick the Habit

Before you begin your mastery of Rule 1, I want to check to see if you have already picked up a bad investment habit. You may think it is a good habit, but it isn't. It is one of the most widely used investment strategies. It comes highly recommended by thousands of investment advisers. Big financial investment firms love for you to practice this investment strategy. You have been trained to believe it is a good investment strategy, a smart investment strategy, and you may even believe it has served you well in years past. But it is an investment strategy I believe you should seriously consider discontinuing. It will keep you from obtaining your goal of making consistent and significant profits in the stock market.

I call it "stock collecting."

Now... you don't know it by that name. You probably know it by its more familiar name: "buy-and-hold." This is the one of the oldest and widest used investment strategies. And in bull markets, like the 1990s, it was a great strategy. You could buy almost anything and see it move up in price. It is amazing how many stock market geniuses there were in the 1990s; and how few there are today. Buy-and-hold works only in bull markets. Unfortunately, we are not always in a bull market.

But before you get all upset with my stand on the buy-and-hold investment strategy, please read on.

I liken the buy-and-hold strategy to being a collector. There is nothing wrong with being a collector. You can collect coins, artwork, vintage cars, and just about anything you can think of. My wife likes to collect cookbooks. We have a house full of cookbooks. She doesn't do a lot of cooking, but if she ever decides to cook anything, she has a library to choose from. And there is absolutely nothing wrong with her desire to collect cookbooks. She gets a lot of pleasure out of it, and I am glad she enjoys it. She has no desire to sell her books or to make a profit from her cookbook collection. She wouldn't know what price to use or if it makes sense to sell any of her collection. She just likes to collect. The important aspect of her collecting is her desire to buy these cookbooks so she can read them, not sell them. If they become more valuable over time, that's great. But selling them is not the reason she buys them. She is a collector, and that's enough.

And there is nothing wrong with collecting stocks, either. You can buy stocks and even have the shares delivered to you. You can frame them. You can put them in a safety deposit box. You can leave them with your broker. But, as a stock collector, you never have a sell strategy. You may tell yourself that you are buying shares of a company because you believe that one day those shares will be worth a lot more than what you paid for them. But the last thing on your mind is selling. You hope the stock will go up in price. You hope the shares won't lose money. You hope you will make a big profit when you sell (although you have no idea when you should sell or at what price). You hope the market will not crash. You hope you will be able to sleep at night.

Maybe you bought the shares because of the wonderful dividend the company pays. Your goal is to generate income from the dividends. Certainly, you would not want to sell those shares that are generating all those great dividends. Those shares bring in a net cash return for you, so selling would be counterproductive to your income goals. Buy-and-hold is a great thing, right?

An even more prevalent reason why investors have a buy-and-hope (oops, I mean buy-and-hold) strategy is their sage financial adviser told them that they need to have a 5- or 10-year investment horizon. Speaking with great authority, these financial advisers pontificate about how it is important not to have a short-term investment strategy. They wax eloquently about the virtues of compounding and reinvestment. Never mind the fact that every quarter they are getting paid a percentage of all you have invested with them, regardless of whether that investment is growing or shrinking. They want you to have your money tied up with them for as long a time as possible. Buy-and-hold is a wonderful, richly rewarding strategy for financial advisers. It rarely is a good strategy for individual investors.

You see, buy-and-hold is, in reality, buy-and-hope. You buy a stock and hope that in 3 years or 5 years or 10 years it will be worth a lot more money. But no one knows the future, especially, your financial adviser. When I hear one of these professional financial advisers say something like, "Well, this stock may not be a great investment in the short run, but if your time horizon is 3 to 5 years, this is an excellent opportunity." How do they know that? They don't know what this stock is going to do in the next 30 days, much less the next 3 to 5 years. They don't know what the economy is going to be in 3 to 5 years. They don't know if there will be a war or a recession. They don't even know if the company behind those shares will still be in business. They are speculating on hope, pure and simple. They haven't got a clue, and in 3 to 5 years, no one will remember if they recommended that stock or not.

But if you don't care about whether a stock's share price will increase or decrease in value in the future, and if you want to buy the stock anyway, then there is nothing wrong with that. However, you must come to terms with the fact that you are not an investor—you are a collector.

It grieves me to see folks tied to a buy-and-hold investment strategy primarily because they have no other option. They don't know how or when to sell, so they are stuck with holding (and hoping) on.

Assuming that you want to be an investor and not a stock collector, I want you to set aside your belief that buy-and-hold is a good investment strategy—at least until you have read my 10 rules. Keep an open mind, and even if you don't quite agree with me to this point, study all 10 rules before you make up your mind about a buy-and-hold strategy.

My 10 rules work great in all markets: bear markets, bull markets, and those awful "trading range" markets. At this writing, markets are flirting with falling into an abyss. No one knows if the market is bottoming or getting ready to plunge downward. Mutual funds have lost billions of dollars for their investors over the past few months. The Nasdaq, Dow, and S&P 500 are off to their worst start in nearly a decade.

But my rules are picking the right stocks and are keeping me in the right amount of cash. We are making money with these 10 rules, when most investors are seeing precipitous and agonizing reductions in their life's savings.

Are you ready to get started? We may be in for a bumpy ride in this market, but these next 10 rules will turn chaos into clarity and big losses into big gains. Turn the page and start down the path to financial freedom, stock market investing success, and, most of all, consistent (and substantial) profits in the stock market!

Hang on tight 'cause here we go!

RULE

1

Think like a Fundamentalist

"If you are going to own a stock . . . it should be a good one!"

$$\begin{matrix} \text{Upward} \\ \text{Trending} \\ \text{Technicals} \end{matrix} + \begin{matrix} \text{Strong} \\ \text{Demand} \\ \text{Fundamentals} \end{matrix} = \begin{matrix} \text{Investment} \\ \text{Success} \end{matrix}$$

Rule 1 is about stock selection. It could be titled the "What to Buy" rule. Buying fundamentally strong companies will lower your risk and improve your chances of generating significant and consistent profits. In this rule, you will learn why *thinking* like a fundamentalist is good, but *trading* like a fundamentalist is bad. In this rule, you will learn how to know *what* to buy, not *when* to buy. You will learn when to buy in Rule 3.

You will learn the importance of stock selection based on some, but not all, fundamentals. You may know a lot about fundamental analysis, or you may have no idea what the term means. Regardless, this is a must-read rule. Don't rush through it, and certainly do not skip it. This is a critically important rule.

When you learn the concept of thinking like a fundamentalist, you will be surprised at how easy and straightforward it is to use that thinking to vastly improve your ability to know just the right stocks to "consider" buying. The key is to own *only* fundamentally strong stocks, but you want to own them *only at the right time.*

You may already use fundamentals in your analysis of a company before buying the stock. If you do, that is good. If you don't, you soon will. Remember, half of your decision making about what to buy is based on fundamentals. The other half is based on technicals, which we will get into in later rules.

Keep this concept in your mind throughout this book: You want to develop a set of rules that will give you a distinct advantage in the stock market. This doesn't mean you have to become a master of everything there is to know about fundamental analysis or technical analysis. In fact, you are better off not becoming too consumed with too much analysis. You could spend dozens (even hundreds) of hours studying a company's fundamentals before you buy stock in that company. But, unless you are a Warren Buffett, where you are buying millions of shares, you really do not have to spend all that much time in your fundamental analysis.

This may seem somewhat counterintuitive. After all, if an investment methodology is good enough for Warren Buffett, why wouldn't it be good enough for any investor? It all comes down to the law of diminishing returns.

Law of Diminishing Returns

This "law" has as its premise that there is a point at which the cost of obtaining additional knowledge becomes significantly higher than the value of knowledge itself. In other words, the effort you would have to expend to find enough additional knowledge about a company will cost you much more than the investment you are making in the company. For a stockholder who is only buying a small fraction of a company's total outstanding shares, the cost of significant additional fundamental research becomes far more expensive than the shareholder will ever hope to make in net total return. Warren Buffett, however, can spend significant effort and cost to analyze every aspect of a company's fundamentals and have very little negative impact on his potential net total return.

As an engineer, I am always looking for the most efficient use of my time. I want to spend the least amount of time possible to extract the minimum level of information required to make an appropriately informed decision about the quality of the fundamentals of a stock.

If you spend too little effort, you will not have the sufficient information to make an intelligently informed decision. This means that you would be putting too much faith in your hunches or what you hear on TV every evening or what your broker told you or what your golfing buddy said. You must do your own fundamental research, and you must do enough to make an intelligent and informed opinion, but don't overdo this research.

Don't spend too much effort, either. Too much research on a company can lead you to buy the company's stock because you have invested so much of your time researching it. You will begin to justify the purchase of stock because, either consciously or subconsciously, you have already invested so much of your valuable time that you will want to justify that effort by owning shares in the company. That is overkill on research. Remember, when you buy shares of stock, you are *not* buying the company, you are buying *only* a tiny fraction of the outstanding publicly traded shares. Don't spend more time researching the fundamentals than it is worth. A little later in this rule, I will give you a list of fundamentals that are easy to research and give you just the right amount of business knowledge of the company to justify making a stock selection decision.

Your Rights as a Shareholder

I often find that investors think that they are actually buying a piece of a company when they buy the stock of that company. Some even think that when they pay their broker for those shares, somehow the company is selling the shares and that the money they paid for the shares actually flows directly back to the company. Both of these assumptions are completely false.

It is true that shareholders are typically granted special privileges, including the right to vote on matters such as elections to the board of directors and the right to share in distributions of the company's income, assuming the company, of its own volition, actually distributes income. However, shareholders' rights to a company's assets are subordinate to the rights of the company's creditors. What this really means is that you, as a shareholder, do not actually own a piece of the company's assets. Do you doubt this? Okay, the next time a company is getting ready for bankruptcy, buy one share and see what you get on the other side of the bankruptcy event. The *only* time you are likely to get anything is when the company goes out of business and liquidates its assets and owes its creditors less than its liquidated value. That almost never happens. What happens, most of the time, is that the company reorganizes under the bankruptcy laws and then issues new stock to new shareholders. The previous shareholders are left with absolutely nothing—no shares, no assets, no refunds, no shares in the new company, nothing. So, don't kid yourself; if you own shares of stock in a company, all you really own are pieces of paper that are bought and sold on stock exchanges based on simple supply-and-demand market forces. But you don't actually own the company.

Why, you ask, is this important to know? It is important because I don't want you to get emotionally tied to a company via its stock. Keep in mind that a share of stock is really nothing more than a derivative of the company.

Derivative

In very general terms, a derivative is just something (in this case, a share of stock) whose value changes in response to the changes in underlying variables (in this case, the company that issued the stock).

There is a misconception that when you buy a share of stock, the money that you pay somehow filters its way back to the company that issued the stock. It does not. This happens *only* when you are a part of the original or subsequent public offering. Once the shares start trading after the public offering event, you are participating in a market where the public is buying and selling shares strictly between the owner and the seller. If the price of a company's stock quadruples in price, the company does not get one dime of that increase unless it issues new shares. Of course, the people who work for the company, including the corporate management, will own shares of the company and they will, just like any other shareholder, enjoy the increase in value of their shares. But the company itself does not get *any* additional cash from the shares that are being traded (bought and sold) on the open market.

This is often confusing when you hear the financial talking heads discuss "market cap." If the market price of a stock drops by 20 percent, for example, you will hear the financial analysts talking about how the company's market cap was suddenly cut by 20 percent, resulting in the fact that the company is now worth so many billion dollars less than it was the day before, or words to that effect. In reality, nothing changed as far as the company is concerned. The actual business operations, the book value, the revenue, the total sales, the products in the pipeline, and the like did not change one iota just because the share price dropped by 20 percent. That 20 percent change was the change in the total worth of all the publicly traded shares of the company. And who owns those shares? Investors do, not the company. So it is the collective group of investors that lost their market cap, not the company. There is an exception to this. When a company uses the stock it owns of its own company as collateral for loans, and then the share price drops, its collateral also drops in value. This can cause a company to experience significant financial distress if that company had its stock highly leveraged (i.e., collateralized).

Market Cap

A measurement of corporate or economic size that is equal to the current market share price times the number of shares outstanding.

Remember, you are just buying and selling pieces of paper that have value only because someone else (another investor) is willing to pay you a certain amount of money for those shares.

The objective of this rule is to teach you how to incorporate a fundamental analysis into your investment strategy and save a lot of time by concentrating on only a small subset of fundamentals that are the most important to consider when you are looking for just the right stock.

Objective

There are several thousand stocks that trade every day in markets all over the world, with over 14,000 at this writing, that trade just on U.S. exchanges alone. When you get ready to add a stock to your portfolio, your objective is to pick the right stock out of this vast sea of publicly traded companies.

But the selection process of trying to pick just the right stock from such a large universe of stocks can be a daunting task. It can seem like you are trying to find a needle in a haystack. Actually, this analogy is true. But in this rule, you will learn that finding that needle (or perfect stock, in our case) is far simpler than you might think.

The first step is to understand that fundamentals really do matter when it comes to finding that perfect stock. But an exhaustive study of a company's fundamentals can be overwhelming and very time consuming. Fortunately, there are very few fundamentals that really matter when you are trying to find just the right stock to consider buying.

Fundamentals Matter—Just Not All of Them

To start this process, I want you to *think like a fundamentalist.* Perhaps you are unfamiliar with the term as it is used in stock analysis and don't know what it means to be a fundamentalist, let alone think like one. But, before I explain what it means to think in this way, I would like to share a story with you:

> At a recent World Money Show, a lady came strolling by the booth, with her eyes cast upward toward the 20-foot banner that spread across the top of our booth. Across the right side it said "Think like a Fundamentalist," and on the left side, it said, "Trade like a Technician." She stopped and pointed up at the sign and asked my wife in a rather indignant tone, "Just what are you trying to say with that statement up there?" My wife turned to look at the sign and asked her which statement she wanted clarified. The lady said, "It's that 'think like a fundamentalist.' Are you telling me I have to be a Christian to invest in the stock market? You need to rethink the way you do your marketing!" Before my wife could respond, the lady walked off.

Fundamentalist

With regard to the stock market, a fundamentalist is someone who uses a company's financials and operations to make trading decisions.

There are a number of great responses I would have loved to give her, but alas, I wasn't there at the time.

Suffice it to say, in the context of this book, the term *Fundamentalist* is someone who examines a company's financials and operations—such as sales, earnings, growth potential, assets, debt, management, products, and competition—for the sole purpose of determining if the company's fundamentals meet the fundamentalist's requirements.

A fundamentalist, then, is anyone who makes a stock investment decision based on the results of analysis of the company's financial condition. This analysis is called *fundamental analysis.* Investors who rely heavily on a fundamental analysis to determine what and when they trade in the stock market are considered *fundamental investors.*

Table 1.1 shows a reasonably exhaustive list of fundamentals.

As you can see, this list of fundamentals can be overwhelming. You could spend many hours researching a company based on these fundamentals before making your decision to buy. Then each time new information comes out on the company, you would have to reanalyze the company again, using all of these fundamental parameters. This would consume many more hours. But you will find that you need to study only very few of these fundamentals to learn all you need to make a stock selection decision. I call this small subset of fundamentals my "Demand Fundamentals." I'll explain more about this smaller subset a little later in the rule.

Nevertheless, think about how much time you would need to spend working on all these fundamentals if you just have 10 stocks in your portfolio. But, what if you have 20 or 30 or more? This could rapidly become way more than a full-time job. You might even have to consider hiring a few MBA graduates to help you!

Faced with this task, far too many investors either ignore fundamentals altogether or they spend way too much time analyzing too many fundamentals. I would never buy a stock without analyzing the company's fundamentals, but I am interested in only a very discrete few fundamentals. If your goal is to buy only stocks that will move up in price, you will want to analyze those parameters that have the biggest impact on driving stock prices higher or lower.

Remember, you are using a fundamental analysis to find those stocks that you will *consider* buying. You should never buy a stock solely based on a fundamental analysis. There are just too many other factors that come into play when picking a stock to buy. My 10 rules in this book will teach you how, what, and when to buy and how, what, and when to sell. Using fundamental analysis as the only criterion to buy a stock means you are leaving way too much to luck that your stock selections will make you money. I don't buy

Table 1.1 General Fundamentals

Total cash	Insider shares sold
Profit margin	Shares held by institutions
Operating margin	Number of institutions holding shares
Debt to equity	Price-to-sales (PS) ratio
Last split ratio	Revenue per share
Trailing price-to-earnings (PE) ratio	Revenue per employee
Forward PE ratio	Net income per employee
Last year's PE ratio	Year-over-year revenue
Trailing PS ratio	Quarter-over-quarter revenue
Last year's PS ratio	Year-over-year earnings
Market cap	Dividend rate
Annual dividend	5-year average dividend
Current dividend	5-year revenue growth rate
Payout ratio	3-year revenue growth rate
Yield	5-year annual income growth rate
Current earnings per share (EPS)	3-year annual income growth rate
Forecast earnings per share	5-year dividend growth rate
Earnings before interest, taxes, depreciation and amortization (EBITDA)	3-year dividend growth rate
Total revenue	Gross margin
Total outstanding shares	Price-to-book ratio
Total shares short	Book value per share
Insider percentage	Last 3 quarters' EPS growth rate
Current inventory	Annual EPS growth rate
Previous year's inventory	5-year average EPS
Institution percentage	5-year EPS growth rate
Return on equity	Price strength
Previous year's net profit	Industry ranking
Total employees	Sector ranking
Short interest ratio	Product pipeline
Short interest percent of float	Competitive advantage
Insider shares bought	

stocks and hope I am going to be lucky. I make money in the stock market because of the 10 rules in this book, not because of luck. I would rather you become a disciplined, thoughtful, smart investor. Plus, you will find that the more you follow a well-thought-out investment strategy based on a solid set of rules, the "luckier" you will become at making money—serious money—in the stock market.

At the beginning of the previous paragraph, I used the word *consider*. It is critically important that you realize Rule 1 is used only to find those stocks that you should "consider" buying when the time is right. Rule 1 will help you determine *what to buy*, not *when to buy*. You will learn *when to buy* in Rule 3. When you learn the concept of thinking like a fundamentalist, you will be surprised at how easy and straightforward it is to use that thinking to vastly improve your ability to select (not buy) the right stocks at the right time.

The key is **only** *to own fundamentally strong stocks, but you want to own them only at the right time.*

So with all this in mind, let's dig in to the nitty-gritty of why fundamentals are important and how to best use them to make stock selection decisions.

Why Risk Can Be Mitigated with Strong Fundamentals

To make consistent profits in the stock market, it is important to consistently measure net total return against the risk you had to take to make that return. All of us want to make the highest return possible for the lowest risk possible. One way to keep risk low is to only own stocks that have the strongest fundamentals. In general, the stronger the fundamentals of a company, the less risk there is that the company will go bankrupt or abruptly change from being very profitable to being very unprofitable.

Risk

The likelihood of a stock's price dropping low (perhaps to zero) can be tied somewhat to the stock's (actually the company behind the stock) volatility (pricing movement) over time. Risk can be extremely subjective and its measurement can depend significantly on the "risk tolerance" of each individual. Risk can be measured quantitatively as well. In this regard, one can generally assume that the higher the quality of a stock's fundamentals, the lower the likelihood that the stock's price will go to zero. On an individual stock basis, risk can be measured by comparing the stock's beta, which is a measure of the stock's volatility in relation to the rest of the market. Risk can also be mitigated or reduced through the use of diversification by industry and sector (see Rule 8). Further, risk can be contained through the use of stop losses (see Rule 4).

Also, stocks with strong fundamentals tend to have lower volatility or beta. Lower volatility generally means more consistent and predictable trends in share price movement. High-quality companies with strong fundamentals also tend to pay higher dividend yields and/or have stronger buyback programs, which add to shareholder value.

Beta

A statistical measure of the relative volatility of a publicly traded equity in comparison to the overall market. The beta for the market is considered to be 1.00. Equities, such as stocks, with betas above 1.0 tend to move with the market, but to a greater degree. Equities with a beta below 1.0 tend to move against or in the opposite direction of the overall market. For example, if the market moves up 10 percent, a stock with a beta of 4 will move up 40 percent, but a stock with a beta of 0.9 will move down 10 percent in that same market.

Shareholder Value

The equity portion of a company's capitalization, which is determined by multiplying the number of outstanding shares by current share price.

By analyzing a company's fundamentals, an investor should be able to make an informed decision about whether buying the company's stock is a good investment or a bad investment. In our case, we want to analyze a company's Demand Fundamentals so that we can make an intelligent, informed decision regarding the merits of owning shares of stock in that company.

We also make a giant leap of faith that analyzing a company's fundamentals provides us with an indication of how strong the company will be in the future. We want to own stock in a company that has the likelihood of strong future growth. We use the fundamental data published by public companies as an indicator of how well the company has done in the recent past, how it compares to its peer group, and how well it will do in the future. It is this future that most interests us.

Knowing how a company has performed in the past is important, but not nearly as important as knowing how a company will perform in the future. Fundamental analysts always use past performance as a guide of future performance. It is this "future performance" that we buy when we buy shares of stock in a company.

Unfortunately, fundamentals tend to be very lagging indicators. For example, the fact that a company reports that it beat street expectations does not necessarily guarantee that it will repeat that feat in the upcoming quarter.

Lagging Indicators

Information or trends that provide historical trends or accomplishments, but do not predict future events.

Street Expectations

The average estimates made by brokers and securities analysts regarding various components (generally revenue and earnings) of a company's fundamentals.

The best you can do with a fundamental analysis is to use the results to compare one company to another or one company to a group (industry, sector, or the entire market) of companies. If you can determine that the fundamentals of a company are improving, and perhaps improving more rapidly than its peers, you can reasonably conclude that the company's stock is potentially worth owning.

It is important to get the most reliable fundamental data available. Investors generally turn to publicly available financial reports, such as the annual 10K and quarterly 10-Q reports, where the actual performance of the company is spelled out in black and white. The numbers don't lie—or at least they shouldn't—and can be used as a basis for making investment decisions.

10-K

A Securities and Exchange Commission (SEC)-required and audited annual report that contains the financial results of the company for the past 12 fiscal months.

10-Q

An SEC-required document that contains the financial results of the company for the quarter, noting any significant changes or events. Usually, but not always, companies will also release forecasts on the expected financial results of future quarters, generally not more than one year into the future.

Keep in mind that even the most recently released reports contain data that are very lagging to the actual operation of the company. By the time a 10-K or 10-Q is published, the company is making material operational decisions that are months, if not years, ahead of the data in these reports. While quarterly and annual reports serve as excellent references of where the company has been, they do little to tell you where the company is going. When you buy stock in a company, the future share price of that stock is directly tied to the future of the company, not its past.

But as lagging as fundamentals are, they still provide an important measuring stick of how well the company has performed over time and in comparison to its peers.

Why I Am Not a Fundamental Purist

I would like to sidestep for a minute to express my differences with the pure fundamentalists, if I may. I am not sure where to delve into this subject, but perhaps now is the best time.

This next statement is not an opinion—it is a fact: The fundamentals of a company do not have anything directly to do with the price of shares of stock for that company.

That statement may surprise you, and for the pure fundamentalists out there, to say that strong fundamentals have nothing to do with the share price of a stock seems ludicrous. They would argue that share price and a company's fundamentals are inextricably connected, that, in fact, there is no other real way to determine share price.

I completely understand this line of reasoning, and on the surface it does seem logical. But if all it took for the share price of a stock to go up was for the company to have strong fundamentals, then ask yourself this question: Why does the price of a company's stock sometimes go down even when the fundamentals have not changed?

If the change in share price is tied only to the quality of the stock's fundamentals, then:

- Investors would only buy stocks with strong fundamentals.
- The share price of fundamentally strong companies would always go up.
- Investors would never lose money on a stock as long as the stock's fundamentals continued to be strong.

This, of course, is absolutely not what happens. The share price of fundamentally strong stocks often does drop in price, sometimes precipitously!

My argument with the fundamental purists is this: since the share price of fundamentally strong companies often moves lower, then higher, and then lower again, without the fundamentals of the company changing, then you cannot rely on fundamentals alone in stock selection.

So just what *does* make the share price of a stock move up or down? Let's look and see.

And Now a Little Physics Lesson

Newton's first law of physics is, "A body in motion tends to stay in motion unless acted upon by an outside force." Now, before your eyes glaze over, this physics lesson is merely to illustrate the importance of strong fundamentals.

Stay with me here—this concept is important. You see, we (you and I) investors have one primary goal (or should have) with regard to investing in the stock market. That goal is to make consistent profits. The problem is: *How* do we achieve that goal?

To solve this problem, the solution is simple: Sell stocks at a higher price than you buy them. Okay, now that we have the problem and the solution, we need to make sure the process used actually gets us to our goal.

Basically, that process (or investment methodology) is to buy stocks at lower prices and hold onto them long enough for them to gain in share price, and then sell them before they retreat back to lower prices.

It follows, then, that if we buy a stock that is moving higher in price, we want that stock to remain in that upward pricing movement long enough for us to achieve our primary goal, which is to sell it before it turns against us and moves lower.

One of the aspects of stocks and their market pricing trends is that the stronger the stock's fundamentals, the harder it is for it to suddenly reverse its upward pricing trend.

Think of it this way: If you consider a stock with superb fundamentals to be a battleship and a stock with weak fundamentals to be a dinghy, and both are headed from lower left to upper right, which one would be easier to turn into a movement from upper left to lower right? You are right—it is the dinghy. A dinghy can turn on a dime; a battleship takes many miles to get it to change direction.

So it is with stocks. The stronger the fundamentals of a stock, the more stable its pricing trend, the more predictive its direction, and the easier it is to make money by capitalizing on those trends. So stick with stocks that have the stronger fundamentals. This strategy will tend to generate more consistent profits through more predictable pricing trends.

Supply and Demand—the *Only* Reason Why Stock Prices Fluctuate

At any given time in the market, there will be a host of stocks with share prices that are trending lower. Some of these stocks will have incredibly strong fundamentals. For example, it is not uncommon for you to find 200 to 300 stocks with very strong fundamentals, but only a few of them have share prices that are climbing. *Your goal is to buy only fundamentally strong stocks when the share price is more likely to move up, not down.*

Strong fundamentals do not guarantee that a stock's share price is going to trend higher in the future. Strong fundamentals are important, but strong fundamentals are not enough of an indicator for you to use to buy a stock. In fact, fundamentals have nothing, directly, to do with the share price of a stock.

Here is why.

Have you ever really thought about what makes a stock's share price move higher or lower? As simple as this may seem to you, I find that most investors don't have any idea why a stock's market price actually moves higher or lower.

They may think, wrongly, that it has to do with a stock's fundamentals, or its management team, or its products in the pipeline, or analyst upgrades and/or downgrades. In fact, none of these reasons "directly" make a stock's share price move higher or lower.

Don't get me wrong. Fundamentals do play an important role in picking the right stock to consider buying, but fundamentals do not determine share price. The company's management team does not determine share price. New products, new discoveries, new markets, and analyst upgrades or downgrades do not determine share price.

There is only one thing that can make a stock's share price move higher or lower. That one thing is directly based on the *demand for shares*. The more investors who want to own more shares, the higher the demand. The fewer investors who want to own fewer shares, the lower the demand. Shares of stock are just like anything else that people buy and sell. You know what I am talking about. You learned it in high school economics class. The more demand for something, the higher the price; the lower the demand, the lower the price.

It follows that if you could predict investor demand, you could predict movement in share price. If you knew that demand was going to fall off, you would correctly expect the stock's share price to move lower. Conversely, if you knew that demand was going to increase, you would correctly predict that the share price is going to move higher.

If you can consistently predict investor demand, you can consistently and accurately predict directional moves in a stock's share price.

So what drives investor demand higher or lower? Actually, there are many things that impact this "supply-and-demand" curve for stock shares, including significant geopolitical and socioeconomic news events. But, aside from the news of the day, investor demand (or the lack thereof) for stock shares can be directly tied to just a few stock fundamentals. Since these fundamentals have the most to do with investor demand for shares, I call these particular fundamentals the *Demand Fundamentals*.

Let's see what these are.

Demand Fundamentals: The Key to Stock Selection

Demand Fundamentals are just a small subset of all the "general Fundamentals" listed earlier in Table 1.1. These very special fundamentals will tell you more about a company more quickly than you might imagine. To illustrate this concept, I want you to pick one of your favorite stocks. Perhaps this is a stock you already own, one that you have previously owned, or one that you are considering buying. Next, go to Yahoo![1] and look up this stock and click on the news or headlines section. Read anything about the stock that includes information on one or more of the fundamentals listed in Table 1.1.

Now, while you are still in Yahoo!, look at the stock's chart and try to match up the date of the news and the price movement of the stock on or near those dates. See which of these fundamentals have the most impact on a change in the price of the stock.

You can spend hours and hours poring over these data, but in the end, you will find that only a relatively small set of fundamentals have the biggest impact on investor demand. Here are my Demand Fundamentals:

- Quarter-over-quarter revenue *growth rate*
- Year-over-year earnings *growth rate*
- Quarter-over-quarter earnings *growth rate*
- 5-year average earnings *growth rate*
- Return on equity
- Dividend yield

To understand why these few Demand Fundamentals are the key to finding great stocks, you have to know why a change in these fundamentals will cause a direct and sometimes significant impact on investor demand.

Investors buy stocks when they believe their investment in the shares will yield a profit at some point in the future. For shares in a company to become more valuable, the company has to become more valuable. By and large, all publicly traded companies are evaluated on one overwhelming yardstick. That yardstick is "growth."

---

[1]Go to http://finance.yahoo.com/ or any web site that provides free stock data and enter the ticker of your favorite stock in the lookup field.

If a company's earnings, revenue, return on equity, or dividend is growing steadily over time, the company is becoming more valuable over time. The more valuable a company, the more investors will demand shares in the company. Hence, the more demand for shares, the higher the share price.

No one wants to own shares in a company that has negative growth rates in revenue, earnings, return on equity, and dividend yield. Negative growth in these areas creates less demand for shares by investors. So, again, the less demand there is for shares by investors, the lower the price for shares of stock.

It is very important to understand that it is not the fundamentals themselves that are as important as it is the *rate of growth* (whether that rate of growth is positive or negative) of those fundamentals.

Rate of Growth

Measured by comparing the change in value over time. For example, quarter-over-quarter earnings growth is calculated by subtracting last year's quarter-ending total earnings from the current year's quarter-ending total earnings and then dividing that difference by last year's quarter-ending total earnings. Here is the example in formula format:

- QELY = Quarter-ending earnings last year at this same time for the then most recent quarterly report
- QETH = Quarter-ending earnings as of the most recent quarterly report

$$\text{Quarter-over-Quarter Earnings Growth Rate} = \left(\frac{(QETH - QELY)}{QETH} \right) \times 100\%$$

I cannot overemphasize that *growth is the key!* It is *not* the actual value of the Demand Fundamental, but rather it is the *rate of change* of that Demand Fundamental from one reporting period to another that we want to use in this analysis process.

Let me give you an example of what I am talking about:

Take two companies, Company A and Company B. Last year, Company A had the best fundamentals of its peer group. It generated a 10 percent net profit. Company B had only a 2 percent net profit growth when it reported last year. From a purely fundamental analysis perspective, ignoring rates of growth, Company A is a far stronger company than Company B. The net value of each of the fundamentals was far better for Company A than Company B.

This year, Company A had another fantastic year. Once again, it had the best fundamentals of its peer group. It generated another solid 10 percent net profit. Company B generated only 4 percent net profit.

So, here is the question: With all other things being equal, which is the better company to own—Company A or Company B? If your answer is Company B, you are right!

You may be wondering why Company B is far better to own than Company A. Let me explain.

Company A had zero *growth* in net profit, whereas Company B *doubled* its net profit. Company B had a 100 percent growth rate in net profit—far, far better than Company A. As such, the demand for shares of Company B will almost always push the price of its shares proportionately higher than for those shares of Company A. Based on pure fundamentals (all of which are listed in Table 1.1), Company A is a far stronger and better company than Company B. But—and this is the key—*investors pay for* **growth.** So the demand for shares of Company B will be stronger than the demand for shares of Company A. As such, the share price for Company B will move higher and much more rapidly than those of Company A.

How to Use Demand Fundamentals to Find the Best Stock

Now that you understand that Demand Fundamentals are the key fundamentals to use when evaluating a stock, the next question should be, "How do I use these Demand Fundamentals to find the best stock?"

Remember, in Rule 1, you are finding *only* those stocks that, if the timing were right, would be good stocks to own. You are *not* to use Demand Fundamentals to determine when to buy, only what to buy.

The process to find the best stocks using Demand Fundamentals couldn't be simpler.

As a reminder, below are the six Demand Fundamentals:

- Quarter-over-quarter revenue *growth rate*
- Year-over-year earnings *growth rate*
- Quarter-over-quarter earnings *growth rate*

- 5-year average earnings *growth rate*
- Return on equity
- Dividend yield

All you have to do is place your universe of stocks in a list, with those having the best Demand Fundamentals at the top, and those with the worst Demand Fundamentals at the bottom. The higher the growth rates, the better. The higher the return on equity, the better. The higher the dividend yield, the better.

Using an Excel spreadsheet for this task makes the process very simple. Table 1.2 shows how I would use these fundamentals in such a spreadsheet.

After preparing a worksheet similar to the above, you only need to sort the columns to find the best stock of each Demand Fundamental.

You can take this one step further by scoring each of the Demand Fundamentals; then merely add up the scores, and then sort from best to worst. Table 1.3 is another example of the same five stocks, but with scores instead of actual values.

Table 1.4 is the same worksheet, but sorted based according to the "Total Score" column.

It doesn't really matter what criteria you use for scoring the Demand Fundamentals, but whatever scoring criteria you use, make it consistent. Then, when you sort your stocks by the total score, you can quickly determine which stocks have the best overall Demand Fundamentals.

Table 1.2 Demand Fundamental Spreadsheet Example

Stock	Quarter-over-Quarter Revenue Growth Rate	Year-over-Year Earnings Growth Rate	Quarter-over-Quarter Earnings Growth Rate	5-Year Average Earnings Growth Rate	Return on Equity	Dividend Yield
Ticker1	50%	20%	18%	12%	20%	0%
Ticker2	–8%	10%	5%	8%	4%	4%
Ticker3	15%	100%	10%	4%	8%	1%
Ticker4	4%	22%	50%	13%	15%	0%
Ticker5	–19%	–4%	–12%	3%	1%	0%

Table 1.3 Demand Fundamental Scoring Example (Unsorted)

Stock	Quarter-over-Quarter Revenue Growth Rate	Year-over-Year Earnings Growth Rate	Quarter-over-Quarter Earnings Growth Rate	5-Year Average Earnings Growth Rate	Return on Equity	Dividend Yield	Total Score
Ticker1	8	4	4	2	10	0	28
Ticker2	0	1	0	1	0	8	10
Ticker3	4	10	3	1	2	4	24
Ticker4	1	4	5	3	5	0	18
Ticker5	0	0	0	0	0	0	0

Table 1.4 Demand Fundamental Scoring Example (Sorted by Total Score)

Stock	Quarter-over-Quarter Revenue Growth Rate	Year-over-Year Earnings Growth Rate	Quarter-over-Quarter Earnings Growth Rate	5-Year Average Earnings Growth Rate	Return on Equity	Dividend Yield	Total Score
Ticker1	8	4	4	2	10	0	28
Ticker3	4	10	3	1	2	4	24
Ticker4	1	4	5	3	5	0	18
Ticker2	0	1	0	1	0	8	10
Ticker5	0	0	0	0	0	0	0

The higher the total score, the better the stock's Demand Fundamentals.

Now that you have mastered the concept of scoring Demand Fundamentals, you next need to apply this to your universe of stocks. As I said at the beginning of this rule, there are many thousands of stocks that are traded on stock exchanges every day.

But, even with all of this scoring and sorting accomplished, you still have a lot of stocks in your universe—too many, most likely. Let's get this universe down to a manageable size.

Reduce the Size of Your Universe

The first step in selecting a stock is to get the list of thousands of stocks down to just a handful—maybe only 30 to 100 stocks that you will concentrate on and from which you will select the one or two new stocks for your portfolio. Before you jump to the conclusion that I am insinuating that this 30 to 100 stocks are all the stocks you will ever have to consider, please understand that this exercise of narrowing down the universe of several thousand stocks to just a handful is something you will need to repeat every time you want to add a new stock to your portfolio. The ultimate, original goal, of using Demand Fundamentals to score and rank your universe of stocks in order to quickly narrow this list down to the one or two stocks that you will consider buying.

Remember, your first job is to find the few stocks out of the thousands that have the very best Demand Fundamentals. A simple and straightforward way to make this comparison is to simply score all the stocks in your universe,[2] and then sort your stocks from the highest score to the lowest score. My universe of stocks is about 6,000. You can see this list and how I score them for free on my web site. Just go to www.10EssentialRules.com, where you can see how I have scored these stocks using the same methodology described in this rule and expanded upon in subsequent rules throughout this book.

When you get ready to pick the 10 or 20 stocks to have in your portfolio, the first step is to *score* your universe of stocks. Make a list of those companies that you want to consider buying shares of stock in and assign a score to each of the Demand Fundamentals for each company, using the scoring system described above.

Once you have determined the scores for each stock in your universe of stocks, the next step is to add up each of the individual scores into a total "Demand Fundamental score." Using a scoring process gives you the ability to then rank the stocks from the highest score to the lowest.

Then sort the total Demand scores from the best to the worst. Of course, your objective is to own only the best. But, remember,

---

[2]Your universe could be 20 stocks, it could be 200, or it could be all the stocks traded in the world. It all depends on how much time you can devote to doing the work required to adequately record and analyze the Demand Fundamentals of a stock.

the fact that a stock has the highest Demand Fundamental score does *not* mean that you should run out and buy it. Quite the contrary—all this last portion of Rule 1 does is to help you identify the companies that are the best to own.

And one more thing: **Don't buy any stocks yet!** You are not yet ready to buy any of these stocks you have just scored. All you have done is determine which stocks you would prefer to own *when the timing is right* to buy them.

You will learn when to buy in Rule 3, but first you will need to learn how to stay clear of overpaying for a stock, which I cover next, in Rule 2.

What You Learned in This Rule

You have completed Rule 1, where you learned:

- That you should own only stocks that are fundamentally strong.
- That a fundamental analysis tells you *what to buy*, not *when to buy*.
- That some fundamentals are more important than others when analyzing a company.
- That it is not fundamentals that make stock prices move higher or lower. Rather, it is investor demand that causes share prices to move higher or lower.
- That there are only a few fundamentals that have the largest impact on investor demand. These fundamentals are called Demand Fundamentals.
- That the single most important aspect of Demand Fundamentals is rate of growth of earnings, revenue, return on equity, and yield, over time.

2

Spend Your Money Wisely—The Value Rule

"Always buy more earnings with fewer dollars."

Industry PE	Is Far More Important Than	S&P 500 PE

When you complete this book, you will be able to build your own world-class portfolio of stocks with confidence. It will be a fluid and dynamic portfolio that will change composition as the market changes. The concepts you will learn here will keep you from losing a lot of money in terrible markets and help you make a lot of money in great markets. You will know what to buy, when to buy, and, most importantly, when to sell. No more guessing—and no more sleepless nights.

Before I get into the objective of this rule, let me share a quick story with you. One day, when I was about 16, I was getting ready to go out with some of my friends. Way back then (in the mid-1960s), a dollar was enough to buy some gasoline and a pretty decent meal at the local drive-in. And I was broke. So I asked my dad a question, and after his response, I never asked again.

I asked, "Dad, do you have an extra dollar?" Of course, my assumption was that he would give me a dollar. But he looked at me and said, "Just what is an 'extra' dollar? I've never seen an 'extra' dollar. What does an 'extra' dollar look like? In fact, I've never even *heard* of an 'extra' dollar." He kept on and on about it. Finally, after he quit driving his point home, I restated my request. I said, "Dad, may I borrow a dollar from you?" His answer was, "Sure," and handed me a dollar for the weekend.

Not only did he drive home the fact that no money is extra and should never be considered insignificant, but that lesson also made me think about every dollar that I have earned since then. That episode in my teenage life stuck with me. Each time I would buy something, I would see those dollars in my billfold and consider the purchase from the standpoint of wise use of my money. Was this purchase being made with "extra" dollars or with important, hard-earned, dollars?

So it is when you buy a stock. I don't want you wasting your money. You should spend your money very wisely when buying stocks. We are after incremental increases in profit wherever we can get those profits. One way to increase your bottom-line profit is not to pay too much for a stock when there is a better choice available.

In Rule 1, you learned *what* stocks to *consider* buying. Here, in Rule 2, "The Value Rule," I will show you how to choose between two stocks, if their Demand Fundamentals are identical.

In building a portfolio of high-quality stocks, you will often find that you have more great stocks to buy than you have room for in your portfolio or money with which to invest. This is a common problem that all investors face at one time or another. Think of it this way: You have two stocks that have identical Demand Fundamentals. In fact, both of these two stocks will give you the same opportunity to move higher in price. Which one will you select? In this rule, you will learn how to pick the better stock based on its relative value, thereby spending your money wisely in the process.

As the "portfolio manager" of your own personal portfolio, you are continually faced with the problem of selecting one stock from a basket of many stocks, each with great Demand Fundamentals and excellent technicals (more on this in Rule 3). You will have to work through a "process of elimination" where you gradually eliminate stocks from your basket of stocks, until you have just the right one.

You will have to compare the Demand Fundamentals, the impact to diversification (Rule 8), the technicals (Rules 3 and 10), institutional ownership (Rule 7), asset allocation (Rule 9), and, as you will learn in this rule (Rule 2), the relative *value* of one stock over another. For this rule, *relative value* is defined by calculating how much it costs per share to buy one dollar of earnings, and then comparing one stock to another based on this relative value calculation.

A simpler way to state this is to compare the price-to-earnings (PE) ratio of one stock to the PE of another. Price divided by earnings tells you the ratio of cost of shares to the earnings derived via the owning of those shares. One of the most important measures of a company is its earnings. You learned in Rule 1 that an important component of analyzing earnings is to measure the *rate of growth in earnings.* In Rule 2, you will learn how to use the combination of share price and earnings to determine which stocks have the best value. As a stock market investor, one of your goals is not to overpay for a stock. If two stocks are equal in all other areas, it is always better to buy the one that has a better earnings value. Another way to say the same thing is to buy the stock with the better PE.

In this methodology, it is not important to only buy undervalued stocks. Quite the contrary, you may often buy relatively overvalued stocks. But when faced with a choice between two stocks that are equally weighted by their Demand Fundamentals, you need a qualifier or criteria by which to choose one over the other. You will need to understand how to use PE ratios in order to make that decision.

When I perform this analysis, I assign a score to each stock's PE. If the stock's PE is significantly higher than the average PE for the stock's industry, I consider the stock to be overvalued. If it is near the top of its industry's PE range, I consider the stock to be highly overvalued. Likewise, if a stock is near the middle of the average PE for its industry, I consider the stock fairly valued. If it is near the bottom of its industry's PE range, I consider the stock highly undervalued. PE ratios that are between fairly valued and highly undervalued are simply undervalued.

Most fundamental based investors will consider PE ratios when analyzing a stock's fundamentals. They *wrongly* assume that a stock with a higher PE is more expensive than a stock with a lower PE. I inserted the word *wrongly* to get your attention and to make a point. Too many investors ignore a key and very important aspect of making a proper value assessment of a stock when comparing one stock to another. A little later in this rule, I will show you how to avoid this error, but if you will indulge me while I sidestep one more time. . . .

Why a Value Investment Strategy Can Be Wrong For You

Before getting into how to use value in your stock selection criteria, let me tell you what I think about being a "value investor."

Value Investor

Someone who likes to buy stocks of companies whose shares appear cheap when compared to current earnings or corporate assets. Value investors typically buy stocks with high dividend yields or ones that trade at a low price-to-earnings ratio (PE), or low price-to-book ratio (PB). Some famous value investors are Warren Buffett, John Templeton, John Neff, and Michael Price.

When it comes to being a value investor, you must first decide how to value a company. The problem lies in being able to adequately determine real value and having access to enough of the right data to make such a determination. There are significant and polar opposite arguments on how to properly determine value and how relative it is to the current market. A lot has been written, and will continue to be written, on whether the market or a stock is overvalued or undervalued. I submit to you that, other than how I use PE ratios in the selection of stocks, it really doesn't matter whether a company or a stock or a sector or an industry or an entire market is undervalued, overvalued, or properly valued.

As bizarre as this may sound, I do not believe in value investing. Not that value investing is wrong. Quite the contrary—for the Warren Buffetts of the world, value investing makes a ton of sense. If you have the resources that Warren Buffett has, where you could know the inner workings of a company, its immediate and long-term prospects, the real ability of the management team, the goals of the board members, the products in the pipeline, the expected acquisitions, the real position of the company in the marketplace and/or the competitive landscape, and a hundred other very important elements associated with making a true value assessment, then, I would say you should be a value investor.

This is not to say that I don't believe in using value to help determine which stock to buy. I just don't rely exclusively on value to make my buying or selling decisions.

Warren Buffett

Warren Buffett (born August 30, 1930, in Omaha, Nebraska) is an American investor, businessman, and philanthropist. He is regarded as one of the world's greatest stock market investors and is the largest shareholder and CEO of Berkshire Hathaway. With an estimated net worth of around US$62 billion, he was ranked by Forbes as the richest person in the world as of March 5, 2008. Often called the "Oracle of Omaha," Buffett is noted for his adherence to the value investing philosophy. In 2007, Buffett was listed among *Time*'s 100 Most Influential People in the World. He also serves as a member of the board of trustees at Grinnell College. Grinnell College has the second-largest endowment of any liberal arts college in the United States.

At one end of the spectrum is the person who is the "less-than-average" investor. He does a mediocre to poor job of investing and is frustrated and unhappy with his choices more times than not. My goal is to help you become the "better-than-average" investor. I want you to be able to make good choices and to be satisfied with them more times than not.

But how do we go about finding the best stocks if all you have at your disposal are the monthly and annual reports on the company, along with an analyst review or two. It is my belief that you do not have enough access to the right kinds of information to adequately be a true value investor.

Many so-called value investors try to outguess the market by using a value analysis to determine which stocks to own. Unfortunately, high-value stocks often fall precipitously in share price. These investors invariably attempt to defend why the market has improperly valued a stock when this happens. Remember, the market is *never* wrong. You will often hear market pundits and stock market mavens rail about how the market has missed something or that the market is wrong. But I say, *"The market is what it is."* To be a successful stock market investor, you must work with the market, not against it. If you ever get to a point where you believe the market is wrong, it only means that you are not in sync with the market.

Is it important to include value in your stock selection criteria? Absolutely. But my advice is to leave the bulk of value investing to the Warren Buffetts of the world. Let's stick with a much more reasonable approach that any investor can use to significantly outperform the market. You will learn how to use one simple element of value, the PE ratio, to make small but important decisions about which one of a small handful of stocks is better to buy when the Demand Fundamentals (Rule 1) are the same for each stock in the group.

With regard to the market, I mentioned above that it is important to "stay in sync with the market." To do otherwise means that the market has moved in the opposite direction to where you thought it was going to move. This happens when you buy a stock, assuming it is going to move higher in price, and it then moves lower in price. This happens when you believe that an entire group of stocks (e.g., energy-related stocks) will move lower and yet that group of stocks defies your logic and moves higher, thwarting your investment strategy in those stocks. When this happens, the result is all too obvious: You will lose money. The only way to make money in the stock market is to buy stocks that the market wants and to sell stocks that the market doesn't want. To make money in the stock market, you must stay in sync with the market.

To know how to stay in sync with the market is not really that complicated. If the market gives you uptrends, then buy long; if the market gives you downtrends, then sell short. You will learn in Rule 10 how to know exactly when the market is signaling you to buy or sell.

Your job is not to try to determine whether a stock is properly valued, regardless of the basis used for that value determination. Your only job, as a stock market investor, is to know when to buy and when to sell. Everything else is just measuring egos and/or listening to value gurus, which is much like watching a stopped clock. It is going to be right twice a day.

However, if you have enough time and research data and can live long enough, a value theory can make some sense. But, since people don't live forever and most investors don't have nearly enough information to really determine a company's value, we are back to realizing that we should basically ignore value investing and take whatever the market is going to give us.

I *will* use value to help make a choice between two stocks with equal Demand Fundamental scores. I am, however, very much opposed to using value as the primary condition on which to make stock investment decisions.

So let me show you how to use PE ratios to help you to select the best valued stocks for your portfolio.

How to Use PE Ratios to Avoid Paying Too Much for a Stock

Most investors recognize that the lower the PE for a stock, the higher its value. In other words, the lower the PE, the less it costs you to, in effect, buy the company's earnings. And, as we learned in the previous rule, investor demand increases almost in direct proportion to a company's increasing rate of growth in earnings.

But when comparing one stock to another, you have to be very careful when using PE as a decision factor.

The key to understanding this concept can be illustrated with a candy bar and a gallon of gasoline.

If I made the following statement to you, you would think I was nuts (and you would be right): "You should buy more candy bars because one candy bar costs a lot less than one gallon of gasoline. The better value, therefore, is in the candy bar."

You know, of course, that it is ridiculous to compare candy bars to gasoline when making a purchase decision. Even if you melted the candy bar into a liquid, so that you could compare one gallon of candy bar to one gallon of gasoline, it still is an asinine comparison. Okay, then, let's compare miles per gallon. How many miles can you travel on a gallon of gasoline, as compared to the number of miles you can travel on a gallon of candy bars? I know—this is getting more and more ludicrous. Why would anyone ever make a buying decision on candy bars or gasoline by comparing the prices of the two products?

But I suspect that is *exactly* what you are doing when you use PE ratios as criteria for buying stocks when the two stocks are totally unrelated.

It is likely that you believe that comparing PE ratios is a good way to determine value, where value is the same thing as saying you are getting more for your dollar. The more earnings you can buy for the same dollar, the better. Right? Yes, that statement is true, but that does not mean you should always buy the stock with the lower PE when comparing one stock to another.

When using PE ratios to make a buying decision between two stocks that have equal or nearly equal Demand Fundamentals, you must make sure the two stocks are from the same industry. It might be reasonable to compare price per gallon of gasoline to the price per gallon of diesel when trying to make a decision on which vehicle to buy. Both of these commodities come from the same industry; in this example, they are both transportation fuels.

This probably makes some intuitive sense to you, but there is a subtlety here that I don't want you to miss.

When buying stocks, the market has determined what it believes to be "reasonable PE ranges" for a certain type (industry) of stock. Investors will buy Google, with a PE of 38, and not bat an eye. But they would never buy JP Morgan with a PE of 38. That would be outrageously expensive. How can that be? Why would investors refuse to buy JPM if its PE was 38 (which it is not, of course) but would (and do) buy GOOG with a PE of 38? After all, a dollar of earnings is a dollar of earnings. What is the difference between a dollar of JPM earnings and a dollar of GOOG earnings? The answer is, "Nothing." Why, then, will investors pay more for a dollar of GOOG earnings than a dollar of JPM earnings?

Sometimes, there is just not a good answer. Most investors would say it is because the ability of Google to generate more earnings in the future is higher than JP Morgan's ability to generate earnings in the future. And that may be true. But, still, we are just talking about what it costs to buy a dollar of earnings, which is what the PE tells us.

Here is the subtlety that I want you to grasp: The market determines acceptable and reasonable PE ranges based on nothing more than what the market will bear to pay. If the market determines that an acceptable PE range for a certain industry is 20 to 200, then a PE of 50 is not unreasonable. However, if the market has determined that an acceptable range of PE is 2 to 20 for a specific industry, a PE of 50 is completely unreasonable.

How to Avoid the PE Misconception

I have a good friend who writes a lot of articles on finance. He is often published in various journals and newspapers and on the Internet. I won't use his name for fear of either embarrassing him or receiving a bad review for my book—neither of which I want. I'll use a fictitious name for reference. I will call him "Joe."

One day, in my e-mail inbox, an article that Joe had written suddenly appeared. I like reading Joe's articles. They are almost always very insightful. In his e-mail, he was reporting on the overbought condition of the market. He was stating a lot of historical statistics on the average PE of the S&P 500. He went on and on explaining how investors were getting sucked into buying more and more expensive stocks because the average PE of the S&P 500 had moved from about 14 to over 16. He was extolling the merits of looking for stocks that had PEs in the subteens.

I was astounded at his complete disregard for the average PE by industry. He had, in one broad stroke of his pen (or, in this instance, keyboard), lumped all stocks into the same comparison criteria, where a stock that had a PE of 10 had a much better value than one of 20 or 30, regardless of its industry. As you will see, he was completely wrong in this comparison.

I wrote him about the article and pointed out what I believe is the fallacy of using the average PE of the S&P 500 as a benchmark from which to compare overvalued or undervalued conditions of equities. I expected him to be somewhat defensive, but his response to my approach to PE analysis was, "Good point."

Don't forget, your objective is to buy and sell stocks at the right time for the right price. So you should only consider buying a stock that has given you a *strong technical buy signal*, which you will learn in Rule 3 and Rule 10; has *strong Demand Fundamentals*, which you learned in Rule 1; and is *supported by strong money flows into the stock's industry*, which is explained in Rule 10.

Your first step is to execute Rule 1 on your universe of stocks. Executing Rule 1 means you have selected a group of stocks that pass your requirement for Demand Fundamentals.

Let's assume you have two stocks with identical Demand Fundamentals and both stocks are in the same industry, but you can buy only one of them. Now, you must choose between them. This is a situation you will encounter often. It is very common that when one stock in an industry is showing strong Demand Fundamentals, there will also be others that are just as strong.

The theory behind Rule 2 is that, with everything else being equal, comparing the PE of one stock to another is a good way to determine which stock is the better value, *so long as both stocks belong to the same industry.* Owning the stock with the better value means you are paying the least amount for the stock with the best Demand Fundamentals.

Now it is critically important that you understand that *all* of the following *must* be true:

1. Both stocks *must* belong to the same industry. If you break this rule, you will be wasting your time doing the rest of the comparison process.
2. You must compare the same type of PE between the two stocks. You can use a trailing PE (last 12 months), the most recently reported PE, or a forecast PE. I like to use the most recently reported PE.

For this discussion, I have selected two stocks that have (as of this writing) identical Demand Fundamentals and both belong to the electrical utilities industry. The names of these two stocks are CEG and GXP. According to their most recent quarterly reports and the then-current market price of the stocks, the PE ratios are:

- CEG: PE of 21.30
- GXP: PE of 17.40

If I could only own one of these two stocks, GXP is a better value since its PE is lower. "Better value" means I can spend less money per share to get the same amount of earnings. The more earnings I can buy with fewer dollars, the better. Why? Because earnings is one of the best metrics for evaluating the strength and growth potential of a company. The more earnings a company makes, the better the company. Investors want to own shares in strong, growing companies. Therefore, investors look at a company's earnings and then how much it costs per share to, in effect, buy those earnings. The objective is to buy the most earnings for the fewest dollars. To know which of two companies has the most value—meaning which of two companies has more earnings for every dollar it costs you to buy shares in those companies—all you have to do is to take the current share price and divide it by the most recently reported company earnings per share (EPS). Once again, the formula is price per share divided by earnings per share equals the "PE ratio." The smaller this number, the better. Why? You want to spend the least amount possible for the most earnings possible. Why? Because the market (the entire community of people and institutions who buy and sell stock) will pay more money for more earnings. *Increasing corporate earnings* is one of the most important Demand Fundamentals.

This probably makes reasonable sense to you, but let me take you through another example. In this case, I am going to—**wrongly and without regard to industry**—select two stocks from entirely different industries (Stock A and Stock B). This, surprisingly enough, is the standard practice of most investors, where they use PE to make a value judgment on a stock, while completely ignoring the fact that the stocks come from separate industries. You see, most investors know only the average PE of the S&P 500, which at the time of this writing is about 16. Because so many of the talking heads on TV use this as some kind of magical standard from which all stocks should be compared, many investors wrongly assume that a PE lower than the average of the S&P 500 is better than a PE that is higher than the average. This misconception will get you in trouble if you let it.

Following is an example that typifies this wrong way of thinking about PEs.

- **Stock A** is from the Internet Information Providers Industry with a PE ratio of 50.
- **Stock B** is from the Health Care Plans Industry. It has a PE of 35.

Based on this information, which is the better stock to buy, assuming they have identical Demand Fundamentals?

If you are thinking that Stock B is the stock with the better value since its PE is far lower than Stock A, you would be wrong.

It is true that 35 is lower than 50, but in the case of Stock B, its peer group (industry) range of PE is from a low of 16 to a high of 35.

For Stock A, its PE peer group range is from a low of 35 to a high of 166. Stock A, with a PE of 50 is near the middle of its peer group and is fairly valued.

Stock B, however, is at the high end of its peer group and, as such, is highly overvalued.

In this example, Stock A with a PE of 50 is a far better value and, therefore, much less expensive than Stock B with a PE of 35.

Looking back to our example using CEG and GXP, the two stocks were from the same industry (electric utilities), and both had identical Demand Fundamentals. By comparing the PE ratios, it becomes even more easily recognizable which one is the better value of the two. We chose GXP because its PE was lower.

So, to this point, when deciding between two stocks of equal or nearly equal Demand Fundamentals, consider only value from within each stock's peer group (industry). Do not consider a PE ratio without considering it from within the stock's industry range of PE ratios.

Why Size Matters

Throughout this rule, there are some underlying assumptions: You do not have unlimited financial resources, and you cannot buy every stock you want to buy.

I am going to assume that, at this point, you have examined your personal finances enough to have made an assessment as to how much money you want to use, put at risk, or invest into the buying and selling of stock in the stock market. You should already know how many stocks you *should* own at any one time, and that number is a fixed number—meaning it doesn't fluctuate all the time.

If these two assumptions (how much money and how many stocks) are not clear in your mind, they will be by the time you finish reading Rule 8 on diversification and Rule 9 on asset allocation later in this book.

Thus, the bottom line is that you *have* to know how much money you are going to use to build your stock portfolio. You *have* to know how many stocks you will possibly own at any one time. You must set these limits and have the discipline to stick to these limits.

Too many investors have no set strategy for buying stock. Many of them just buy a stock based on how much money they are comfortable spending at that particular time. I have seen individual investors who own stocks in over 100 different companies. They are overwhelmed with the number of different companies, and have no idea how to manage such a large group of stocks.

You may be in this position right now—too many stocks and too little time. After you read this book, you will know exactly how many stocks you need to have in your portfolio, and you will know exactly which kinds of stocks to own at any one time. Then, as you manage your world-class portfolio, you will find many situations where Rule 2 will help you choose between two similar stocks because you cannot own both of them.

Building a Bridge over the Colorado River and Why It Matters to Your Investment Strategy

Each year when we attend the Las Vegas Money Show,[1] we get to drive over Hoover dam. We have driven over the dam many times, but the sheer size and stark landscape surrounding the beautiful Lake Mead never cease to amaze me.

As you may know, a bypass bridge[2] is being built by the states of Nevada and Arizona and the U.S. federal government, just downstream from the dam. It is scheduled to be completed in 2010. At this writing, the bridge is just beginning to take shape.

The project is a civil engineer's dream, and even though I much prefer investing in the stock market to building bridges, I must confess that every time I drive down into that canyon and see the enormous structure being built, I am envious of the engineers involved in the project. Just this year (2008) we drove over the dam and saw the amazing spectacle unfolding.

You may be wondering why I would bring the topic of building of this bridge to your attention. It is because the building of this bridge is an excellent analogy to what I am teaching you in this book.

---

[1]The MoneyShow provides forums for stock market and financial market information.

[2]The present route of U.S. 93 uses the top of Hoover Dam to cross the Colorado River. U.S. Highway 93 is the major commercial corridor between the states of Arizona, Nevada, and Utah; it is also on the North American Free Trade Agreement (NAFTA) route between Mexico and Canada. U.S. 93 was identified as a high-priority corridor in the National Highway System Designation Act of 1995. The traffic congestion caused by the inadequacy of the existing highway across the dam imposes a serious economic burden on the states of Arizona, Nevada, and Utah.

You see, each of these 10 rules must be considered integral building blocks to a total investment strategy and methodology. To single out one of these rules to the exclusion of the others would be like attempting to just build a highway across the Colorado River canyon below Hoover Dam without any support or structure to hold it up.

This is a great picture to illustrate my point (see page 51). You can see they have just completed the last of the columns that will support the highway from the foundation poured into the solid granite face of the canyon. And just below that foundation, you see the next step beginning. This is where they are slip-forming the massive arch that will extend from one side of the canyon to the other. Undoubtedly, they will be positioning other columns between the arch and the deck of the highway above. This is truly an engineering marvel.

But, just like this structure must be methodically constructed, with one careful step after another, so are we constructing an investment strategy and lifelong methodology for making consistent profits in the stock market.

To bring this point home to Rule 2, we have just learned why and how to properly use PE ratios as a part of your stock selection process. It would be no more right just to use this rule by itself than it would to use just the part of the bridge you see in Figure 2.1. If the engineers quit at this point on the bridge, it would be useless. If they said, "Let's just concentrate on these wonderful columns and ignore the great arch that is now being built," a bridge would never span the chasm. Before we will be able to drive across this bridge, all the components must be completed and tied together in proper order and with the proper dependency one upon the other.

Just like the engineers who are building this incredible, towering structure, you are now building your structure for investment success. There are 10 major components. Each one is required and each one is dependent upon the other. Do not consider any one of these rules to be not as important as another. Just like the building of the massive arch across the canyon, that part of the bridge might be the most challenging. But the lowly piece of rebar buried in the base of one of the column foundations is no less important to the total success of the final structure. Read and study these rules with that in mind. When you complete these 10 rules, you will see how beautiful a structure you have created, but instead of something that you drive across, it will be something you can use to drive into the future as you build and grow your financial security and create wealth for you and your family.

I would like to suggest that you go get a second cup of coffee before we start the next rule, where I will teach you how to trade like a technician. You have absorbed a lot so far and would probably like to have a fresh mind. Go ahead. It's okay with me!

What You Learned in This Rule

A lot of the work that you must do in your quest to find the right stock to buy at the right time is the work of deciding between two stocks that have nearly identical Demand Fundamentals. In this rule, you learned:

- That most investors do not have enough information or time to be a true value-type investor.
- That value, as defined by a stock's PE ratio, is a very good way to choose between two stocks of equal or nearly equal Demand Fundamentals.
- That with all other things being equal, such as the Demand Fundamentals, you should always pick the stock with the lower PE. However (and this is very important), you should only compare PEs of stocks from the same industry.

RULE 3

Trade like a Technician

"If markets were efficient, traders would be extinct."

$$\text{Pricing Trend} + \text{Historical Volatility} = \text{Market Timing Success}$$

In this rule, you will learn how to use pricing trends to tell you when to buy a stock. In Rules 1 and 2, you learned how to find the stocks that you should *consider* buying. In Rule 3, you will learn the first step in timing your purchase. This is the "When to Buy" rule.

If you are new to technical analysis or have never used technicals to make trading decisions, all you have to know is that to trade like a technician, you have to learn how to read charts.

Technical Analysis

Technical analysis is a method of evaluating stocks by relying on the assumption that the future share price of those stocks can be predicted by analyzing historical share price charts, historical volume charts, sector pricing charts and industry pricing charts. Technical analysis ignores fundamental analysis. The assumption is that historical charts have well-defined patterns that are highly correlated to future pricing trends.

(continued)

> Thereby, trading decisions (buy, sell, short, or cover) can and should be made predicated on the likelihood that future pricing trends will repeat the same or similar patterns the stock exhibited in the past.

Just as there are fundamental analysts, there are also technical analysts. These two camps have a certain distain for one another. Fundamental analysts don't believe in charting. They don't believe in the concept of telling the future by looking at the past. And technical analysts believe that fundamental analysts are out of touch with reality. They say that regardless of the fundamentals, the pricing trend could go lower or higher. Technicians want to buy on the way up and sell on the way down, regardless of the fundamentals.

I believe you have to look at both the fundamentals *and* the technical aspects of any stock you are about to buy or sell. You will gain insight in both approaches that significantly outweigh just using one or the other. The whole, in this case, is far more valuable than the sum of the parts.

This rule focuses on the technical aspect of stock selection.

Perhaps you already consider yourself an accomplished "technician." That is great! Some of this rule will be somewhat remedial for you, but not all of it. I use a technical approach to charting stocks that you likely will not have seen before. It is not complicated, but it has an uncanny ability to time when to buy and when to sell short. Even if you have used technicals in your stock investment methodology for years, you should read this rule. It is likely that regardless of how much you know about reading charts, trends, oscillators, patterns and triggers, you still need this rule.

But if you have never stepped foot into the technical waters, we will cover the elementary components of technical trading so you won't be left out. In Rule 10, which is the rule on timing the market, we will take this process to a whole new level of sophistication and understanding. Don't jump ahead, though. This book is meant to be read from the front to the back—one rule at a time.

Putting This All in Perspective

I know you just spent the last two rules learning why fundamentals matter. Now, as we move on to why technicals matter, I want to make sure you are not confused.

I don't believe that fundamental analysis and technical analysis methodologies are mutually exclusive. Indeed, I believe that one without the other is like trying to swim with one arm while letting the other arm hang by your side. It is possible to swim with one arm, but it is very difficult. However, making stock investment decisions based on both a fundamental and a technical analysis is much like watching a champion swimmer, with both arms used to propel the swimmer forward. Indeed, swimming with two arms is far more efficient and effective than just doubling the success of swimming with one arm. Likewise, using both fundamentals and technicals, the stock market investor has the best chance of being more efficient and effective at generating significant and consistent profits.

With regard to technical analysis, I believe in "keeping it simple." My technical analysis methodology is simple but powerful. It is something you can actually use without spending hours and hours of studying and screening and doing what-if scenarios.

As we go through them, you will learn:

- The basic theory of technical analysis.
- How to build a simple but powerful trend line.
- How to determine what triggers a buy and what triggers a sell short, from a technical perspective.

Types of Technical Analysis Systems

All technical analysts have one simple objective: to determine whether a stock's price is going to move up or down in the future based on how that stock's price has moved in the past. It doesn't matter which technical system you learn or which technical charts you follow. In the end, your goal will be the same as all other technicians: you want to figure out the pricing trend of a stock. Will that trend be down so that a short trade makes sense? Or will that trend be up so that a long trade makes sense? Will the stock stop moving higher so that it can be sold at or near its top? Or will the stock stop moving lower so that it can be covered at or near its bottom?

There are many types of technical analysis systems, including:

- **Accumulation/distribution index:** A momentum indicator that tries to gauge supply and demand by discovering if investors are generally "accumulating" (buying) or "distributing" (selling) a certain stock by identifying divergences between stock price and volume flow.

- **Average true range:** A technical analysis indicator developed by J. Welles Wilder, based on trading ranges smoothed by an N-day exponential moving average (EMA).
- **Bollinger bands:** Developed by John Bollinger, Bollinger bands (lines) are plotted above and below the 21-day moving average of a stock's price. These upper and lower boundaries factor in two standard deviations (about 95 percent) of the price movement over the previous 21 days.
- **Breakout:** A chart pattern used to indicate a rise in a stock's price above its resistance level (such as its previous high price) or a drop below its support level (commonly the last lowest price).
- **The Dahl theory:** The primary theory used in this book for technical analysis wherein a stock's pricing trend is determined by how its week-ending closing price crosses a 10-week moving average of week-ending closing prices, with this trendline shifted forward in time by three weeks.
- **Hikkake pattern:** A technical analysis pattern used for determining market turning points and continuations. It is a simple pattern that can be observed in market price data, using traditional bar charts, or Japanese candlestick charts. The pattern is comprised of a measurable period of rest and volatility contraction in the market, followed by a relatively brief price move that encourages unsuspecting traders and investors to adopt a false assumption regarding the likely future direction of price.
- **Moving average convergence/divergence (MACD):** A technical analysis indicator created by Gerald Appel in the 1960s. It shows the difference between a fast and slow EMA of closing prices.
- **Momentum and rate of change:** Simple technical analysis indicators showing the difference between today's closing price and the close N days ago.
- **Money flow in technical analysis:** Typical price multiplied by volume, a kind of approximation to the dollar value of a day's trading.
- **On-balance volume:** A measure of volume distinguished as to whether trades take place on rising prices or on falling prices. Technical analysts consider great volume on rising prices bullish because it indicates the possibility that large traders are accumulating investment positions in a security.
- **Price activity (PAC) charts:** PAC charts are unique in the way they represent "volume" (the number of shares traded every

day), where compound estimated volume data at each price level is plotted and color-coded.

- **Parabolic stop and reverse (SAR):** A method devised by J. Welles Wilder Jr., to find trends in market prices or securities. The concept draws on the idea that time is an enemy, and unless a security can continue to generate more profits over time, it should be liquidated.
- **Pivot point:** A means to calculate resistance and support levels, which are, in turn, used as visual cues to execute trades. Pivot point calculations provide traders with objective visual benchmarks, which some use to predict price changes.
- **Point and figure charts:** Show trends in price by, in theory, filtering out the "noise" (unimportant price movement) and focus on the main direction of the price trend and are used for longer-term price movements.
- **Relative strength index:** Developed by J. Welles Wilder, it is a financial technical analysis oscillator that shows price strength by comparing upward and downward close-to-close movements.
- **Rahul Mohindar oscillator (RMO):** A type of technical analysis developed by Rahul Mohindar of Viratech India, which detects trends in financial markets and is designed to work on open-high-low-close charts.
- **Stochastic oscillator:** A momentum indicator, introduced by George Lane in the 1950s, to compare the closing price of a commodity to its price range over a given time span.
- **Trix oscillator:** Shows the slope (i.e., derivative) of a triple-smoothed exponential moving average. The name *trix* is from "triple exponential." It was developed in the 1980s by Jack Hutson, editor of *Technical Analysis of Stocks and Commodities* magazine.
- **Williams %R oscillator:** Developed by Larry Williams, it is a technical analysis oscillator that shows the current closing price in relation to the high and low of the past N days (for a given N).

Reading Charts Is Easy—Finding the Right Chart to Read Is the Key

Don't be daunted by the idea of learning to read charts. If you have never attempted to follow or even understand the concept of technical analysis, reading and studying this rule will turn you into an excellent stock technician.

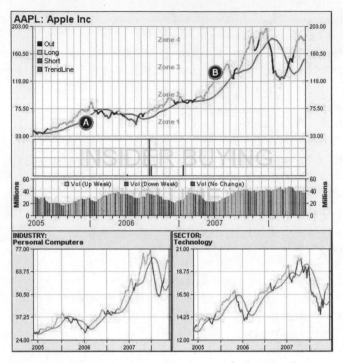

Figure 3.1   AAPL

Figure 3.1 shows a simple technical chart[1] of AAPL (Apple, Inc.).

This is an easy chart to read, and as we move further into the book, the charts don't get much more complicated.

The black line (Circle A) is just a 10-week moving average trend line.

10-Week Moving Average Trend Line

A 10-week moving average is simply the average of 10 week-ending closing prices, which is updated weekly by dropping the oldest value (11 weeks ago) and then adding the newest value (this week's

---

[1]The author does not make any representations or warrants as to the accuracy of the charts in this book. The reader should consider these charts as examples only and not infer any suggestions from the author that any of the equities so referenced should be purchased. The charts and/or commentary on any equities should not be considered as a recommendation to acquire or divest shares of the stocks and/or companies referenced.

week-ending closing price) and recalculating the average. A 10-week moving average of stock would be calculated by summing the last 10 week-ending closing prices and then dividing that total by 10. Each week, you would drop the oldest week-ending closing price and calculate the average with the most recent 10 week-ending closing prices in its place. Then, you take that average and plot it on the chart for that particular week.

This moving average is based on the average of the 10 most recent week-ending closing prices of a stock. The only complicated thing I do with this trend line is slide it from left to right three weeks. This "time-shifted" trend line has proven to provide a better basis from which to judge when a stock is in an uptrend or a downtrend. You can use any trend line that you like.

Trend Line

A widely used technical analysis approach to judging when to buy and sell stocks. I do not use a trend line for timing when to sell. I use it to time when to buy or sell short. Trend lines can be used to identify positive and negative trending charts, where a positive trending chart is a chart that moves from the lower left (lower prices) to the upper right (higher prices). A negative trending chart is one that moves from the upper left (higher prices) to the lower right (lower prices). One of the major purposes of trend lines, in addition to signaling when to buy or sell short, is to signal when a stock's pricing trend has changed direction. Stock market investors want to own stocks that are trending from the lower left to the upper right. They want to sell and then sell short stocks that stop that trend and begin moving from the upper left to the lower right.

The other line in Figure 3.1 is the week-ending closing price of the stock (see Circle B). You will note, from the legend on the chart, the week-ending price line can be "out," "short," or "long." Here's what this means:

- When the week-ending price line (see Circle B) is black, it means that there is not enough of a directional movement in

the price line to determine if it is trending higher or lower. When the line is black, it means:
- You should not buy the stock.
- You should not sell the stock short.
- If you own the stock, you should sell it.
- If you are short the stock, you should cover it.

• When the pricing line is above the trend line and changes from black to light gray, it is your signal that the stock has likely moved into a trend from lower left to upper right and that it is also likely that this upward sloping trend will continue for some time. This is a good time to buy the stock.

• When the pricing line is below the trend line and changes from black to light gray, it is your signal that the stock has likely moved into a trend from upper left to lower right and that it is also likely that this downward sloping trend will continue for some time. This is a good time to short the stock.

There are many nuances to technical charts, and we will get into some of the more important nuances in Rule 10. But, the concept is no more complicated than this: You will time when you buy and when you sell short by watching how the price of a stock moves above or below a moving average trend line.

When the stock's price moves above the trend line, you buy.

When the stock's price moves below the trend line, you sell short.

It doesn't get a lot more complicated than that. But there is one thing that I must hasten to add at this point:

You don't have enough information to start buying and shorting yet. This is just Rule 3. You *must* put all 10 rules in your investment methodology before jumping into the market. It would be a big mistake for you to chart a few stocks, slap on a trend line, and start buying and shorting. Please wait until you have finished this book before putting any of these rules to work.

Building the Right Technical Chart

I use stock charts to tell me when to get *in* the market (buy or short), but I use what I call my "Intelligent Stop Loss®" formula, which is registered with the U.S. Patent Office, to tell me when to get *out*. You will learn all about the Intelligent Stop Loss® formula in Rule 4.

The objective of every technical chart of every technical system ever created is to achieve the following goal: to tell you the difference between normal volatility and a change in direction of a stock's trend line.

Every investor wants to buy stocks that are trending higher in market price, and for stocks that are trending lower in market price, investors will either sell their long positions or sell short.

It doesn't matter what technical system you use; your goal will be to know the difference between normal volatility and a change in the overall direction of the stock's market price.

Remember: Never buy a stock unless it is supported by *both* technical *and* fundamental buy signals.

As I mentioned earlier, you can use any technical system you want, but you *must* use one. A little earlier in this rule, you learned how to read a very simple chart of AAPL. You learned about a moving average and what to do when a stock's price moved above or below the moving average trend line.

Take a look at the chart in Figure 3.2. This is an expanded set of charts all pertaining to AAPL.

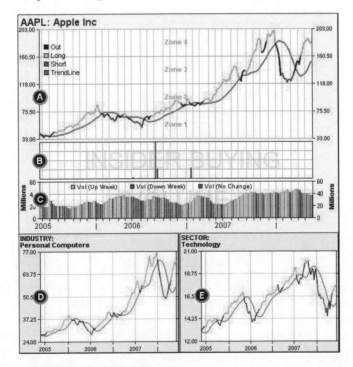

Figure 3.2   Expanded AAPL Charts

You will notice that the main (upper) chart is a three-year chart of Apple just like the chart you saw in Figure 3.1. There is a lot of information in Figure 3.2, including:

- Main chart (see Circle A)
  - On this chart, you can see the week-ending market price of AAPL, including the 10-week moving average (trend line). This chart gives you an easy-to-read indication of whether you should own the stock, have a short position in the stock, or have no position in the stock at all. As you learned earlier in this rule, depending on whether the stock's week-ending price is above the trend line or below it, you will immediately know if you should have any position in the stock. If the week-ending share price is sufficiently above the trend line, it is okay to own the stock. If the week-ending share price is sufficiently below the trend line, it is okay to short the stock. If the week-ending share price is not sufficiently above or below the trend line, then you should not be long or short the stock. The indicators are:
    - Out: This means you should have no position in the stock and the price line is black.
    - Long: This means the chart supports you holding a long position in the stock. When the price line moves from black to gray and is above the trend line, the chart is giving a "buy signal."
    - Short: This means the chart supports you holding a short position in the stock. When the price line moves from black to gray and is below the trend line, the chart is giving a "sell short signal."

Long Position

A long position means that you have purchased the stock with the expectation that its market price will increase over time. Unlike shorting a stock, the most you can lose is your entire investment if the price of the stock goes to zero.

Short Position

A short position means that, through your broker, you borrow shares of the stock and immediately sell those shares, where you are paid by the buyer. Your assumption is that the market price of the shares will decrease over time. At some point in the future, hopefully, when the market price of the stock is lower, you buy the same number of shares you borrowed earlier and give them back to your broker. You get to keep the difference between the price at which you sold the shares immediately after you borrowed them, less the amount you paid to buy them back. Of course, if the stock's market price moved higher after you borrowed the shares and sold them, you would have to buy the shares back at a higher price to return the shares to the broker. In a short sale, it is possible to lose more than your total investment.

- There are four zones. These zones are nothing more than the difference between the stock's lifetime highest share price and the stock's lifetime lowest share price, adjusted for splits. The purpose of the zones is to give you an idea of how much risk you might want to make in a stock, as follows:
  - It is not a good idea to short a stock in the lower half of Zone 1. This is because the stock is very near its lifetime lowest low and it is less likely that it will, in the near future, start making lower lifetime lows.

Splits

When a company decides that it wants to have more shares of its stock available to the public, but at a lower price, and it does not want to issue new shares, the company will execute a corporate action in which all of its outstanding shares are divided into multiple shares. For example, if a company splits its stocks 2-for-1, it means that for every share currently traded on the open market, those shares immediately double in number, while at the same time, the price per share is reduced by 50 percent. Although the number of outstanding shares doubled, the total dollar value of the shares remains the same compared to presplit market price. This is because no real value was added as a result of the split.

○ You have the greatest potential for return if you buy a stock that is giving a buy signal as it moves out of Zone 1 into Zone 2. This is because the stock has already demonstrated that it can trade at the top of Zone 4, so its potential for growth is greater in Zone 1, 2, or 3 than in Zone 4 (with the following caveat).

○ Winners tend to win. Stocks that give buy signals in the upper half of Zone 4 tend to move higher making new lifetime highest highs. In upward trending markets (see Rule 10), buying stocks that are giving buy signals in the upper half of Zone 4 can produce exceptional returns.

- Insider buying (see Circle B)
  - You will learn more about insider buying in Rule 6.
  - This chart does not have an enumerated y-axis, which means the vertical black bars are relative only. The total number of shares being bought by insiders is not nearly as important as knowing if there is increasing or decreasing amounts of insider buying.
- Weekly trading volume (see Circle C): Watching the total trading volume of a stock can tell you a lot of information about the strength or weakness of the stock's market pricing trend. I use a 10-week moving average volume on this chart. The details on this chart are:
  - The black vertical bars are "up volume," which tells you that the stock's market price is increasing as the trade volume of shares increases. You can infer from this action that the market likes this stock and it is likely that more investors are buying more shares. At the very least, you know that more shares are being traded at increasing market prices.
  - The light gray vertical bars are "down volume," which tells you that the stock's market price is decreasing as the trade volume of shares decreases. You can infer from this action that the market is not as enamored with the stock at that time, as more investors are selling more shares. At the very least, you know that more shares are being traded as the stock's market price is decreasing.
- Industry chart (see Circle D): There is no better gauge of how strong a stock's pricing trend is than by knowing how a particular stock's "market" is moving. The two best indicators of how

bullish or bearish the market is, with regard to a specific stock, are its industry and sector (more on sector later). The industry chart is a chart of the average market price of every stock in a particular stock's industry. In this case, with AAPL, the industry is "personal computers." This industry chart includes:

- A 10-week moving average trend line, which charts the average week-ending closing price of all the stocks in the personal computers industry.
- If the average price of every stock in the industry is above the trend line, the industry is considered in "bull mode." This means that more money is flowing into this industry than out of it. It means that more investors have a positive opinion of this industry than a negative opinion. In a "rising-tide-lifts-all-boats" environment, a stock that has strong Demand Fundamentals and is in a technical buy mode, and has its industry and sector in bull mode, you should draw the conclusion that there is a lot of pressure on your stock's market price to move higher. This is the exact scenario that you must look for in your technical analysis.

- Sector chart (see Circle E): Although I put more emphasis on a stock's industry bull or bear mode condition, certainly it is a major positive when *both* the stock's industry *and* sector are bull mode. In Figure 3.2, Circle E, you can see AAPL's sector chart. The sector chart is a chart of the average market price of every stock in the stock's sector. In this case, AAPL's sector is "technology." This sector chart includes:
  - A 10-week moving average trend line, which charts the average week-ending closing price of all the stocks in the technology sector.
  - If the average price of every stock in the sector is above the trend line, the sector is considered in "bull mode." This means that more money is flowing into this sector than out of it. It means that more investors have a positive opinion of this sector.

By looking at Figure 3.3, you get information telling you when to get into a stock for either a long or a short trade. You also can use this chart to help you determine your exit strategy (more on this later).

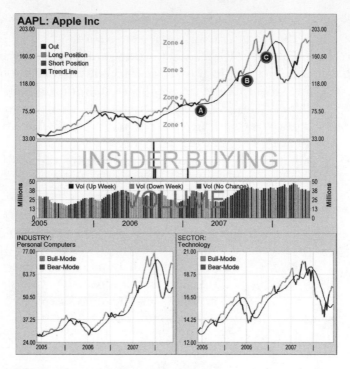

Figure 3.3   Using Technicals for Entry Positions

When a stock's week-ending closing price moves above the trend line, the stock has given a technical buy signal. When the week-ending closing price moves below the trend line, the stock has given a technical short sell signal.

I use a stop loss strategy (The Intelligent Stop Loss® strategy, which will be covered in Rule 4) to tell me when to sell a long position or cover a short position. When a stock triggers its stop loss setting, the color-coding on the market price line turns black. This signifies that no trend has been sufficiently established and the stock should not be owned or shorted.

I realize all of this can be a bit overwhelming, especially since these charts cannot be easily reproduced without a program designed and written specifically for this technical strategy. However, you can get very close to this same concept by using a standard 50-day moving average and Bollinger bands set at a 50-day time period and utilizing one standard deviation. Of course, all of these charts are available for free on my web site.

So, the actual concept is very simple:

- You execute a buy or short sell when the weekending price of the stock crosses the trend line. You buy when it crosses the trend line moving up and you short when it crosses the trend line moving down.
- You sell when the stock's price reaches the stop loss price.

Allow me to summarize to this point. In Rule 1, you learned how to pick the stocks that you would consider buying if the timing was right. In Rule 2, you learned how to spend your money wisely when buying a stock. And here, in Rule 3, you are learning how to know when it is the right time to buy one of the stocks you have selected in Rules 1 and 2. You should consider buying a stock only if it has strong Demand Fundamentals and its price has moved above the trend line.

Avoiding the Noise of the Market

As you develop your trading and investment strategy, you have to make very singular decisions (buy, sell, sell short, cover) from a plethora of inputs. These 10 rules provide you with an easy-to-follow road map that simply and effectively navigates your decision-making process through a maze of data to a decision that you can believe in and that will give you confidence in your stock selections.

As investors, we are inundated with information. The vast amount of information spewing from the Internet, TV, radio, newspapers, analysts, company financial reports, and the like is indeed mind-boggling. Buried within that mountain of data is the knowledge that we seek. The knowledge that we want is: what to buy; when to buy; and, most importantly, when to sell.

If you master these 10 rules, you will learn how to emotionally distance yourself from the minute-by-minute, hour-by-hour, or day-by-day vagaries of the market. You will learn how to rapidly turn overwhelming amounts of information into a few wonderful and critically important nuggets of knowledge.

For example: If the market is up 200 points on Monday and down 300 points on Tuesday, then back up 50 points on Wednesday, such whipsaws and volatility in the market can overwhelm your emotions. One day, you think you should be in the market; the next day, you think you should be out, only to reverse that thinking again the following day.

I consider the cacophony of information and the volatility of the market during the week as just so much "noise." Making investment decisions in the din of so much market noise invariably leads to mistakes.

A far better approach is to let the markets close for the week, gather your data, and then, in the relative peace and quiet of the weekend when the market sleeps a couple of days, take a deep breath and make your trading decisions. Look at the week's market activity from the perspective of the weekend.

When determining trends, it is extremely important to remove noise from your decision making. Noise can drown out important considerations. Noise can be the news, analyst upgrades and downgrades, talking heads on TV, geopolitical events, and a host of other distracting information. Noise can also be a part of your data, in the form of outliers and volatility. It is important to reduce and/or eliminate as much noise from your analysis as possible.

It doesn't matter that much what happened day to day; what really matters is how each stock's price changed from end of week to end of week.

I want you to get away from watching too much stock market news. Turn the TV off. Follow these rules and then spend more time doing things other than worrying about buying and selling stocks.

In these 10 rules, you are going to learn how to build a world-class stock portfolio and make all your trades and set all the upcoming week's exit strategies in a couple of hours on the weekend. The rest of your life should be devoted to more important activities than the stock market.

Reading the Tea Leaves

Depending on the technical system that you follow, reading and understanding technical charts can be more than a bit difficult. You saw that long list of methodologies espoused by different theorists, and that is a list of only the most recognized ones. Frankly, I have never seen a complex technical system provide any significant increase in net total return over what you get from simple technical methodologies. In fact, I have seen just the opposite. Often, the simpler the technical approach, the more easily you can detect strong trading signals. The better the trading signals, the more profit you will move to the bottom line.

Outlier

An outlier is a number in a set of data that is much larger or smaller than most of the other numbers in the set. With regard to the 10 Essential Rules, all trends are based on week-ending closing share prices. Other than the impact to stop loss settings and/or stop loss orders, intraweek share prices are irrelevant. Likewise, intraweek market movement is irrelevant. The only data used for trend analysis is based on the week-ending closing prices for stocks and/or markets. Wild changes in prices during the week are considered to be irrelevant and not to be included in the development of trend lines. These atypical stock or market prices are considered as outliers and are ignored.

Now, let's move back to the chart in Figure 3.2 on AAPL. I want you to pay close attention to the three circled letters on the chart.

At Circle A, the stock's price began moving up toward the trend line. A couple of weeks later, the stock crossed the trend line, which triggered a buy signal. Immediately after buying the stock at Circle A, it is critically important to set your stop loss order. We will discuss how to calculate and set your stop loss prices in Rule 4.

You would continue to own AAPL until Circle B. At that point, the stock's market price dropped enough to trigger the stop loss and you sold.

Then, about three weeks later you bought AAPL again, when it once again moved back up above the trend line. Then, you held onto your position until the stock once again triggered its stop loss setting at Circle C.

In this way, you "stair-step" your way along with the stock as it moves higher and higher in price. But you avoid the catastrophic collapses (note the sell-off just to the right of Circle C) through the judicious use of stop loss settings.

With the 10 Essential Rules, you will not be buying at the bottom and selling at the top. Rather, you will be buying *near* the bottom and selling *near* the top. Attempting to buy at the bottom is like trying to catch a falling knife. Most of the time you will get "cut" (lose a lot of money), and, therefore, you should try to avoid the habit of trying to buy at the bottom.

In this example, you would have bought the stock at Circle A for about $80 per share and sold it at Circle B for about $120 per share. This is a $40 per share gain in about five months. That is about a 50 percent net gain, which annualizes to more than 120 percent. Then, from Circle B to Circle C, you made another $40 per share in just over two months for a net gain of 33 percent and an annualized return of almost 200 percent!

Calculating the Annualized Return

To calculate the annualized return, divide the time the investment is held into the total number of trading days in the year, which is about 255 trading days. Then multiply that number by the net return. The assumption is that you could make the same amount the rest of the year that you did in the shorter time period.

The point to all of this is that these are profoundly powerful charts that can give you an excellent indication of when to buy and when to short. Of course, you want to buy only fundamentally strong stocks, but the timing of your buying and selling is how you make consistently significant profits in the stock market! I know it works. I've done it. And you can, too!

What You Learned in This Rule

This is the rule that tells you when to buy. You learned:
- That it is good to own fundamentally strong stocks that have upward pricing trends.
- That reading and understanding technical stock charts will provide the knowledge of which direction a stock's price is most likely to move.
- Why it is important to remove market and data noise from your decision-making process.
- How to build and read a technical stock chart.
- How to recognize when a stock triggers a buy signal and when it triggers a short sell signal.

4

The Stop Loss Rule

"The best stress reliever is a smart stop loss order!"

$$\begin{array}{ccccccc} \text{Unrealized} & & \text{Stop Loss} & & \text{Less} & & \text{More} \\ & + & & = & & \text{and} & \text{Consistent} \\ \text{Gain} & & \text{Order} & & \text{Stress} & & \text{Profits} \end{array}$$

So far you've learned the principles of Demand Fundamentals, the use of the price-to-earnings (PE) ratio to avoid buying expensive stocks, and the basis of technical analysis for picking the right time to open a new trade. In Rule 4, you will learn the *right time to exit* a position. This rule could be called the "Intelligent Stop Loss®" rule.

I believe this is the single most important concept of my approach to the market. There should be a huge star beside Rule 4! I have been "saved" from many whipsaw sessions in the market by using this strategy.

Whipsaw

Whipsaw is when a stock's market price makes a quick move up or down, followed by a sharp price change in the opposite direction. All too often, an investor will buy or short on a whipsaw event, only to be fooled by the sudden reversal and have to either sell or cover. Generally, an investor gets whipsawed when he or she does not follow a rigid set of rules that governs the timing of entry and exit points.

The objective of this rule is to hold onto a stock as long as it is making you money. "Making you money" is the important phrase here. It means you want to hold onto a stock as long as the stock's market price is trending or moving in the direction that provides an increasing level of unrealized gain.

Unrealized gain is the profit you would make, in terms of real dollars, if you were to sell a stock at the current market price, if the current market price is more than you originally paid for the stock. Conversely, "unrealized loss" is the actual dollar amount you would lose if you were to sell the a stock at the current market price, where the current market price of the stock is less than the amount you originally paid for the stock. With regard to short selling, unrealized gain is the difference between the amount of the stock when you borrowed and then sold the shares, compared to the current market price of the stock if you were to buy the same number of shares and return those shares to your broker, assuming the current market price of the stock is less than the price you sold them for when you initiated the trade. Conversely, in a short sale, if the price of the stock has moved higher from the price at which you sold the shares when you put on the trade, the difference would be your unrealized loss.

The term *unrealized* means that until you close the trade—meaning until such time as you sell a long position or cover a short position—you have not actually made or lost any money, regardless of the difference between the price of your stock when you initiated the trade and just prior to your closing the trade. An unrealized profit becomes a real profit when you close out a trade and convert your shares back to cash. The same is true for an unrealized loss. The loss does not become "real" until you close out of your position in the shares originally bought or sold short.

A good approach is to maintain two sets of running totals on your portfolio. One is based on the total value of your portfolio (including cash and equities) at the beginning of each year or month or inception and the current value of your portfolio (including cash and equities). This would give you the total profit or loss, including all unrealized gains and losses. The other is based purely on net cash gain or loss. In this approach, you assume the beginning value was zero and you track only the net result of closed trades. If a closing trade results in a net cash loss, your net cash profit moves lower. If a closing trade results in a net cash gain, your net cash profit moves higher.

Both of these views of your investment strategy are important. The best way to measure real performance of your stock market trading prowess is to monitor your net cash gain or loss. All unrealized gains and losses can change in a moment, depending on the vagaries of the market.

Now that you've read this rather lengthy explanation, let me summarize our main objective: If you are long in a position, you want the stock's pricing trend or directional movement, to be higher and higher. You want just the opposite if you are short in a position. The key to making consistent profits in the stock market is to only keep stocks in your portfolio that are making you more and more money and get out of those that are not making you money.

Going with the Flow

I believe there is an ideal place or position to maintain when you are riding in an up-and-down market (which is pretty much the kind of market we have all the time). I often use the following story to illustrate why it is important to not get out of sync with the market.

I want you to pretend that you are a wildebeest roaming the great African savanna. You are not by yourself. In fact, you are mingling with a great herd of wildebeests. You have only one enemy in life: the lions.

The herd starts moving across the savanna. It just so happens to be moving from the lower left to the upper right. This makes you very happy. You are happiest when the herd is moving from the lower left to the upper right and you are the saddest when the herd moves from the upper left to the lower right.

But, at the moment, life is good. You are with the herd, and the herd is moving in the right direction. Now, let me ask you a question: Just where in the herd are you? Are you out at the edges of the herd or are you right in the middle?

If you are a smart wildebeest—and I am sure you are way above average—then you are not out at the edge of the herd. Why do I think that? Because I am sure you already know what happens to you if you hang around at the edge of the herd. The lions can pick you off!! Those at the edge of the herd are always fearful and are never too sure when the herd will suddenly veer one way or the other and leave them alone and stranded in the midst of lion country.

You, of course, know of these things and you are smart to stay as close to the middle of the herd as you can.

Now, let's move this story from the world of imagination to the real world of stock market investing. As a stock market investor, you want to move with the herd.

I know, you've been told that to make money in the market, you *must* think outside the box, you must be a maverick, you must *not* have a "herd" mentality—you *must not* go with the herd.

I suspect that the *only* reason you have ever been told that is the person doing the talking has no idea how to follow the herd and how to make money by following the herd. In fact, that person has no idea how to take advantage of market movements, so they try to justify their complete lack of being able to capitalize on market movements by saying you shouldn't follow the market.

I tell you it is imperative that you learn how to follow the market. It is the *only* way to consistently make superior profits and maintain significantly low risk. I know how exciting it is to be a maverick and run outside the herd. But, if you want to be a maverick and run around outside the herd, you had better be fast and tough. The lions, which in this case would be a sudden reversal in your stock's pricing trend, are anxiously waiting for you.

It is far better to be safe and secure by staying in the middle of the herd and to own stocks that are moving higher because that is the direction the herd is moving, than to be outside the herd where the risk is high and results can be financially life threatening.

For those mavericks who are reading this section and are, perhaps, scoffing at this approach: You may be saying to yourself that you can't live with the low return of safe and secure stock investments. Know this: These 10 rules are designed for **a low-risk approach to investing**, but with a net total return goal of 20 percent per year or more. There are not many so-called mavericks making 15 percent to 20 percent every year. With these 10 rules, you are not guaranteed to make 15 percent, 20 percent, or more per year, but you will consistently make more profit and have many years in which you will exceed your 20 percent goal with these rules.

I believe in low risk, but I also believe in high returns. The investment strategy contained within these 10 rules will achieve that objective.

Remember, when your stocks are moving in price from the lower left of the chart to the upper right, you want to be in the middle of the herd. There is no sense in your trying to find a stock that the market has little, if any, interest in and does not have a herd of investors pushing its price higher and higher. No, your job is to find those high-quality stocks that the whole herd ("market") likes and buy in early, then ride merrily along with the market as long as your stock's price is moving higher.

But, unlike the wildebeest, which must stay with the herd or be eaten by the lions, when the herd suddenly veers away from pushing your stock from the lower left to the upper right, you can simply sell your shares for a profit and look for another opportunity where the herd has picked up another high-quality stock and is once again pushing it from lower left to upper right.

The key, of course, is to know when your stock has reached its upward pricing trend and is about to start moving lower. All stocks cycle through times of upward pricing trends and lowering pricing trends. No equity's pricing trend moves in a straight line. Some of that movement is just normal volatility. Some of that movement is directional, where the general pricing trend of the equity is moving either lower, higher, or sideways. Every investor wants to know the difference between normal volatility and a change in pricing trend.

Sideways

When a stock trades "sideways," it means that the stock is trading in a very narrow range over an extended period of time.

Investors would be far wealthier if they could distinguish the difference between normal volatility and a complete change in direction of the pricing trend of a stock. As you learned in Rule 3, every technical system ever created or that ever will be created has this as its primary goal—to know the difference between volatility and a change in direction of the pricing trend of a stock.

To make a profit, you must first buy a stock and then sell it later at a higher price, of course. Traveling with the herd can help you do this, while at the same time lower your risk. But, surprisingly, many investors do not consciously know the primary reason why they buy stocks. You should know one very important—might

I say, critically, important—aspect of stock market investing. You *must* **know the** *primary* **reason to own a stock**. Without this knowledge, there is no sense in your buying one more share of stock.

The Primary Reason to Own Stocks

You never make money by *buying* **the right stock at the right time; you can make money only by** *selling* **the right stock at the right time.**

Let me repeat that . . . "You *never* make money in the stock market by buying the right stock at the right time—never. You will make money in the stock market *only* by selling the right stock at the right time—and, of course, at the right price!"

How many times have you heard someone say, "If only I had bought that stock at the right time, I would be rich by now" or "It seems like I always buy the really good stocks at the wrong time"?

Stock market investors are, typically, obsessed with buying the right stock at the right time. They seem to think that is all that matters. They read financial journals. They go to investor conferences. They attend local chapters of investment groups. They listen to the talking heads on the financial news channels. They subscribe to investment newsletters. They do this for one reason and one reason only: They want to find the next stock to buy. They are obsessed with and singularly focused on buying the right stock at the right time. They do this because they think that the most important part of stock market investing is to buy the right stock at the right time because they think that is how they will make a profit and grow their portfolio. *They could not be further from the truth!*

Buying the right stock at the right time only exchanges your cash for shares of equal value. Nothing has changed except that you had cash and now you have shares. You haven't made a dime or lost a dime; you have only exchanged one asset for another of equal value—dollars for shares.

Stock market investors generally spend a lot of time thinking about *what* to buy. Most investors will research companies before buying stock in those companies. They will go through no small amount of fundamental and technical analysis to make their final decision on what to buy. This is a good thing, although they often spend too much time researching the wrong data (review Rule 1).

Once they have bought a stock, they believe the hard part is done. But it isn't. These investors sit back and wait for their wonderful stock picks to climb higher and higher. Sometimes, their stocks do move higher and higher; other times, those stocks tend to move lower and lower. Still other times, they move sideways—up for a while and down for a while.

The single most important thing you can do as a stock market investor is to sell your stocks at the right time. In fact, **the number one reason for buying a stock is to sell that stock, and sell it at a profit.** Why? Because you never actually make a dime out of a trade until you sell. Anything else is just a paper profit or a paper loss. Holding a stock with unrealized gains does avoid having to pay taxes on the gains, but the problem is that those unrealized gains can turn into unrealized losses if you do not sell at the right time. Bernard Baruch is often quoted as saying his biggest fault with his investing strategy was that he "always sold too soon."

Bernard Baruch

Bernard Baruch was born in Camden, South Carolina, to Simon and Belle Baruch. He was the second of four sons. His father, Simon, was a German immigrant of Jewish ethnicity who came to the United States in 1855. He became a surgeon on the staff of Confederate general Robert E. Lee during the American Civil War. In 1881 the family moved to New York City, and Bernard Baruch graduated from the City College of New York eight years later. He eventually became a broker and then a partner in the firm of A. Housman and Company. With his earnings and commissions he bought a seat on the New York Stock Exchange for $18,000 (approximately $458,000 in 2007 dollars). There, he amassed a fortune before the age of 30 via speculation in the sugar market. In 1903 he had his own brokerage firm and had gained the reputation of "The Lone Wolf on Wall Street" because of his refusal to join any other financial house. By 1910, he had become one of Wall Street's financial leaders.

Sources: © 1999 South Carolina Business Hall of Fame and *Bernard M. Baruch*, James Grant (John Wiley & Sons, Inc.)

You can't do much with unrealized gains or losses. You can't spend unrealized gains. You can't buy a new house with unrealized gains. You can't buy food or pay for college with unrealized gains. Sure, you might be able to borrow money against unrealized gains, but that is extremely risky. Remember, the key to making consistent profits in the stock market is to consistently turn unrealized gains into realized gains. That event occurs only when you sell at a profit.

However, most investors will tell you that they either have no idea when to sell or that selling is the single most difficult decision they try to make. There is almost always a lot of second-guessing and what-if'ing going on when an investor is trying to decide whether to sell some or all of a stock.

So, what can you do when a stock you own moves against you? Do you always know if it is better to sell or to hold on a little longer? After you finish this rule, you will *always* know exactly what to do after you have bought a stock. You will *always* know exactly when to sell.

But When Should I Sell?

Each year, I speak to literally thousands of stock market investors. These investors come in all varieties. Some are seasoned investors, some are buy-and-hold investors, some just own mutual funds, some are day traders, some are momentum traders, some are just getting started. Some have millions of dollars in the stock market; some have only a few thousand. But, invariably, most of them all have the same common problem—they have no idea when to sell.

Learn this rule and you will *always* know when to sell. You see, knowing when to sell is a formula. It's not guesswork, and it's not closing your eyes and grimacing while saying to yourself, "I hope I'm doing the right thing, selling this one!" You do not have to rely on emotion or gut feeling. When you come to realize that your number one reason for buying a stock is to sell it, and start using the formula in this rule to determine the sell price, you will become a far, far wealthier investor.

In fact, if I've helped you realize already that the only reason to buy a stock is to sell it, then you are more than halfway to mastering this rule. But most investors never know for sure when it is time to sell. They ask themselves:

- Have I made enough profit?
- Should I sell before this week's earnings report?
- I'm losing money on this stock, but should I hold onto it a while longer and see if it goes back up?
- I've lost so much on this stock, how can I sell now and lose so much of my investment?

- Analysts say the price target on this stock is much higher than it is now. Should I hold on?
- I bought this stock based on its strong fundamentals. The fundamentals haven't changed, but the stock is down 20 percent from where I bought it. Should I hold on? Should I buy more and average down my net basis?
- I really like what this company does. I don't understand why the stock's price keeps dropping. Should I sell now or wait for the market to turn around?
- I can't believe I am in the same predicament again. I bought this stock at the top and now have lost so much. I know that just as soon as I sell it, the stock will rebound. What can I do to get out of this horrible and expensive vicious cycle? It happens to me every time.

Of course, before you sell a stock, you must first buy it. Most investors would use one or more of the following reasons to buy a stock:

- The stock has great fundamentals.
- The stock has perfect technicals.
- The stock has been highly recommended by very knowledgeable investors.
- The stock has an incredible dividend.
- The stock has the number one rating in the current *Investor's Business Daily* 100 Top-Rated Stocks (IBD-100).
- Your broker said this stock is a "lock."
- It is the best stock to own according to all 10 of the rules in this book!

Yet, none of the above constitutes the ***primary*** *reason to buy* a stock. Some of these reasons are valid for picking the best stock to buy, but none of these reasons are why you should buy any stock.

Think about this: At the very beginning of this book, I listed many reasons why people invest in the stock market. Regardless of those reasons, each reason has one real goal: to make a reasonably high rate of return on capital at an acceptable level of risk.

To make money in the stock market, there are only two critical steps you must take:

1. Buy shares.
2. Sell those shares at a profit.

This is a simple credo, but it is extremely important. I want you to commit these next few words to memory and make them a part of your investment DNA:

The *only reason* to buy a stock is to *sell it!*

Investment DNA

DNA is the material inside the nucleus of cells that carries the genetic blueprint of life. In this case, "investment DNA" is the blueprint of how an individual invests in the stock market.

After reading this rule and applying this rule to your current investing strategy, you will *never* worry about when to sell again—*never!*

Timing Is Everything

This strategy will achieve two very important goals for you:

1. Mitigate downside risk.
2. Provide you with the right price and the right time to sell.

If the primary reason to buy a stock is to sell it, it naturally follows that you need to know the timing and the price for selling. Not every stock you buy is going to move higher in price. Even if you follow 100 percent of the rules in this book, some of your stock picks will be losers. An extremely important part of making consistent profits in the stock market is to know when to get out of losing positions.

Let's assume you have just selected a stock for several reasons, one of which is the stock's pricing trend is moving higher and you want to take advantage of that trend. You buy the stock and then it begins to move lower and lower, reversing its up trend to a downtrend. What do you do? First of all, how do you even know if the trend has reversed? How do you know it is not just a normal downtick in volatility?

If a stock's price drops due to normal volatility, it will soon recover and continue to move upward. However, when a stock's pricing trend reverses, it can show a very similar price drop as it moves against you.

Moves Against You

"Moves against you" means that the price of the stock moves in the opposite direction of your objective. For long positions, the stock's price moves lower. For short positions, the stock's price moves higher. In either case, the stock's pricing trend is moving against you.

Take a look at Figure 4.1. This is a chart of Apple, Inc. over about a three-year period between 2003 and 2008.

As you can see from the chart in Figure 4.1, AAPL had a spectacular rise from Circle A to Circle B, as its price moved from about $80 to $200. Let's assume you decided to buy this stock just as it moved above $180 a share. For the next week or two, the stock continues up to nearly $200 and you are ecstatic. Then, it drops back to $118 (Circle C). What should you do?

Of course, looking back in time, you can easily see you should have never bought at $180, but at the time, there was nothing but

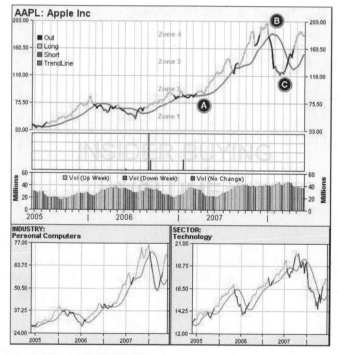

Figure 4.1   AAPL (2003–2008)

good news about the company and the analysts were all saying the stock could easily move much higher. The best time to have bought AAPL was at Circle A, but how could you have known that at the time?

Now, look at the same chart in Figure 4.2, but this time let's dig a little deeper.

First, let's assume you bought AAPL in August 2007 (Circle A). From there, AAPL moved from $120 to over $190 (Circle B) in about two months, and then dropped back to near $160 two weeks later. At that moment, could you have known if this were just "normal" volatility or the start of something much more significant, like the crash of AAPL between Circle C and Circle D?

Of course, anyone looking at the chart in Figure 4.2 can see that you should have sold at the top (Circle C), but when the stock was at the top, there was nothing but positive and exciting reasons to stay in. There was nothing to keep it from going higher, perhaps to 300 or more. Plus, when it began to sell off in October 2007, it recovered

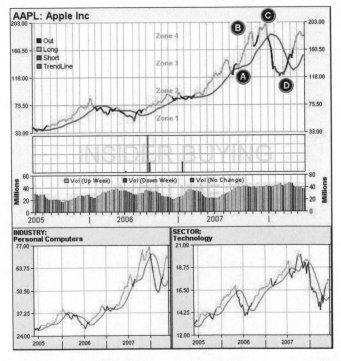

Figure 4.2   AAPL: When to Sell?

completely and went on to a new lifetime high at Circle C, so you convinced yourself that such a reversal could happen again at any time. Yet, from its high in late 2007 to early 2008, you saw all of your wonderful profits disappear. Now, you are in despair and want to sell, but you convince yourself that you really haven't lost anything. It is still a great company and it is bound to move higher again soon. And perhaps it will.

AAPL moved all the way back up above $180 at the end of this chart. From Circle A to Circle C, you would have made over 40 percent. But from Circle C to Circle D, you lost more than 40 percent. Do you really want that kind of risk in your portfolio, where you have to suffer through 40 percent losses? Wouldn't it have been better to have bought AAPL at Circle A, sold it at Circle B, bought again just to the right of Circle B, and then sold at Circle C? Even better would have been if you had shorted AAPL at Circle C and then covered at Circle D, where you bought again. You could have made 40 percent on the way up to Circle C, made another 40 percent on the way down to Circle D and yet another 40 percent between Circle D and the end of the chart.

My point is this: Timing is everything when it comes to making money in the stock market. And the best way to time your entry and exit points is through the use of a technical system that tells you when to buy and when to sell.

In Rules 1 and 2, you learned *what to buy*. In Rule 3, you learned *when to buy*. Now, in Rule 4, I want to show you *when to sell*.

The Intelligent Stop Loss® Strategy

To avoid getting trapped into a stock that is falling in price, you should always have a predetermined sell price—*always!*

To accomplish this task, I strongly recommend using a stop loss strategy. You need a stop loss order that meets the following criteria:

- The price at which you can be relatively certain that the stock has reversed direction and is moving lower.
- The maximum amount of loss you are willing to accept and not be outside your loss comfort zone.
- The price you are willing to take for your stock after you have made a profit.

Stop Loss Order

A stop loss order is an order to close out the trade (sell if long or cover if short) if and when the stock touches or moves through the stop loss order price.

Loss Comfort Zone

"Loss comfort zone" is the percentage of loss you can experience on a single trade and not lose sleep at night. Every investor has a loss comfort zone, beyond which they will become very fearful and uncomfortable. If you invest in the stock market, you are guaranteed to lose money on some trades. This will be true even if you follow each of the rules in this book explicitly. Some investors can tolerate a loss of 20 percent on a single trade; some 10 percent; some as much as 50 percent or more; and some as little as 5 percent. Only you know your own loss comfort zone and your tolerance for loss.

All stocks move up and down during a trading week. This movement is normal and considered nothing more than volatility. The key is to know the difference between normal volatility and when to exit a trade. To know this, you must be able to differentiate between normal volatility and a change in the directional pricing trend of the stock.

As I have said many times, the goal of every technical timing system, regardless of its methodology, is to know the difference between volatility and a change in direction. The Intelligent Stop Loss® strategy provides that critical piece of knowledge. The formula is predicated on the following assumptions:

- Stop loss orders are to be set one week at a time.
- The data used in the formula are based on the most recent trading week and the most recent trading year.
- Historical volatility will not appreciably change in the upcoming 5 trading days when compared to previous 52 weeks of historical volatility.

- If a stock's market price moves below the calculated stop loss price, that stock's pricing trend has reversed from moving higher to moving lower.
- If a stock's market price moves above the calculated stop loss price, for short positions, the stock's pricing trend has reversed from moving lower to moving higher.

This stop loss formula has been tested and back tested in thousands of real-world trading situations. It has been tested on both stocks and exchange-traded funds (ETFs) and in markets spanning more than 50 years. Will it give you the perfect stop loss setting every single time? No. But will it make you a wealthier investor and lower your risk in the market at the same time? *Yes.* Remember, the stock market is a very dynamic and often imperfect process where buyers and sellers are often swayed as much or more by emotion than fact. Inconsistencies, surprises, breaking news, geopolitical and economic eruptions abound, and always will. Data are often lagging indicators, and trends become more difficult to predict. But trends do develop, and the investor who ignores these trends is likely to be the poorer for it.

The objective of my stop loss formula is to provide the best stop loss order price to use for the upcoming week, such that it will stay just below normal volatility, but high enough to provide a backstop exit price should the stock deviate from its normal level of volatility.

This stop loss formula is exceptionally accurate and will provide you with a consistently reliable stop loss price that will help protect your downside and yet give your stocks enough room to fluctuate in normal volatility actions.

Volatility and the Stop Loss Price

I have mentioned normal volatility several times. It is important that you clearly understand the importance and relationship between volatility and the stop loss price. Every stock has a fairly consistent pattern of volatility. Stocks do not, normally, go from a weekly price fluctuation of 5 percent that has been consistent for the past 12 months and then suddenly move into a consistent volatility pattern of 20 percent. One of the major assumptions behind this stop loss formula is that once a stock has established a normal level of volatility, it will not abruptly change unless it is changing its pricing trend. This means a stock that is in an uptrend will stay in a consistent level of volatility as long as it continues in the uptrend.

Conversely, a stock will tend to stay within a consistent level of volatility when it is in a downtrend as long as that trend continues lower. Further, it is very likely that a stock will break out of a consistent volatility pattern when its pricing trend reverses, where uptrends move into downtrends and downtrends move into uptrends.

Statistically, we can calculate how much a stock is likely to move up or down (i.e., expected move), within one standard deviation of the mean of the past 12 months of a stock's volatility. The first step in determining the expected move (EM) is to calculate the historical volatility (HV):

Standard Deviation

Standard deviation is the root mean square (RMS) deviation of values from their arithmetic mean.

$$HV = \frac{(52 \text{ week high} - 52 \text{ week low})}{\text{Average } (52 \text{ week high} + 52 \text{ week low})}$$

Once we have calculated the HV, we can next calculate the EM as follows:

$$EM = \text{Stock Price} \times HV \times \left(\frac{\sqrt{5 \text{ Trading Days}}}{\sqrt{252 \text{ Annual Trading Days}}} \right)$$

In the above formulas, the following definitions are applicable:

- The "Stock Price" is the most recent week-ending closing price.
- The "5 Trading Days" is the upcoming trading week.
- The "252 Annual Trading Days" represents the most recent 12 calendar months.

Once the EM has been calculated, you are then ready to calculate the best stop loss price for the upcoming trading week as follows:

- Stop loss for long positions = previous week's lowest low − EM
- Stop loss for short positions = previous week's highest high + EM

There are several important observations and conclusions about this methodology that you should understand:

- Stop loss calculations are performed after the closing bell for the most recent week.

Closing Bell

The closing bell for the week references the day and time when U.S. equity markets close for the week.

- The stop loss price is valid for the next trading week, with the exceptions noted in Rule 10.
- Stop loss prices should be adjusted for known dividends/ distributions that would cause the price of the stock to be adjusted by the amount of the dividend or distribution.
- If a stop loss calculation results in a price that is lower (in the case of long positions) than the previous week's stop loss price, the new stop loss price should remain at the previous level. In other words, do not lower your stop loss settings. For short positions, the opposite is true.

Let's look at an example. In this example, we will use Google, Inc. (see Figure 4.3). You will notice that at Circle B, the week-ending closing price went from light gray to black, well above the trend line. This means that you would have stopped out (and, therefore, sold) at that point. You learned in Rule 3 to time your entry into a new position based on, among other things, the crossing of the week-ending closing price above the trend line. This is what happened at Circle A.

However, your exit from GOOG becomes totally dependent on the stop loss. Using 2007 as an example trading year, you would have bought at Circle A, based on Rule 3. You would have sold at Circle B, based on Rule 4. Then, you would have bought again

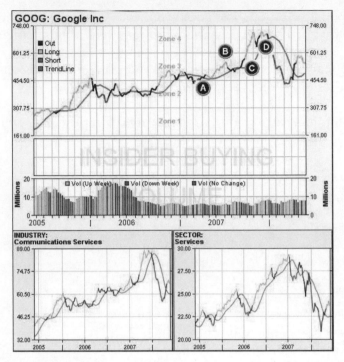

Figure 4.3   GOOG Historical Chart

at Circle C and, subsequently, sold again at Circle D. See details on these trades in Table 4.1.

Had you just bought at Circle A and held on indefinitely, you would have made very little money and suffered through some very tough times. You are far better off to get in when the market tells you and get out when the stock's price violates its stop loss setting.

Back to the wildebeest analogy. As long as the herd is moving your stock's price in the right direction, you stay right in the middle of the herd. This would be, for example, between Circle A and Circle B; or between Circle C and Circle D. But when the herd moves in the wrong direction (see Circle B and Circle D), you merely sell your shares and wait for a time when the herd once again starts pushing your stock from the lower left to the upper right.

Important: You get into a position using the trend line; you get out using the stop loss.

Table 4.1 shows GOOG's pricing and stop loss calculations for 2007.

Table 4.1 Trading Action on Google, Inc. for 2007

Week-Ending Close Date	Week-Ending Closing Price	Week's Lowest Low	Expected Move	Stop Loss	Percent of Price	Status	Net Profit
1/5/2007	$487.19	$459.86	$29.49	$430.36	6.05%		
1/12/2007	$505.00	$481.20	$30.56	$450.63	6.05%		
1/19/2007	$489.75	$486.74	$29.64	$457.09	6.05%		
1/26/2007	$495.84	$477.29	$30.01	$457.09	6.05%		
2/2/2007	$481.50	$477.81	$29.14	$481.51	6.05%		
2/9/2007	$461.89	$461.50	$27.96	$484.70	6.05%		
2/16/2007	$469.94	$455.02	$28.44	$484.70	6.05%		
2/23/2007	$470.62	$462.06	$28.48	$482.06	6.05%		
3/2/2007	$438.68	$438.68	$26.55	$501.81	6.05%		
3/9/2007	$452.96	$437.00	$27.42	$492.93	6.05%		
3/16/2007	$440.85	$439.00	$26.49	$481.75	6.01%		
3/23/2007	$461.83	$440.63	$26.85	$481.75	5.81%		
3/30/2007	$458.16	$455.00	$22.52	$481.75	4.92%		
4/5/2007	$471.51	$452.12	$23.18	$471.50	4.92%		
4/13/2007	$466.29	$462.24	$22.92	$466.39	4.92%		
4/20/2007	**$482.48**	**$468.15**	**$23.72**	**$444.42**	**4.92%**	**Bought at Circle A**	
4/27/2007	$479.01	$475.55	$23.55	$451.99	4.92%		
5/4/2007	$471.12	$464.17	$23.16	$451.99	4.92%		
5/11/2007	$466.74	$461.00	$22.94	$451.99	4.91%		
5/18/2007	$470.32	$457.41	$23.12	$451.99	4.92%		
5/25/2007	$483.52	$466.72	$23.26	$451.99	4.81%		
6/1/2007	$500.40	$477.27	$24.07	$453.19	4.81%		
6/8/2007	$515.49	$497.59	$26.63	$470.96	5.17%		
6/15/2007	$505.89	$498.69	$26.13	$472.55	5.17%		
6/22/2007	$524.98	$504.24	$27.12	$477.12	5.17%		
6/29/2007	$522.70	$519.46	$28.13	$491.32	5.38%		
7/6/2007	$539.40	$519.46	$30.31	$491.32	5.62%		
7/13/2007	$552.16	$540.01	$32.14	$507.86	5.82%		
7/20/2007	$520.12	$509.50	$31.03	$507.86	5.97%		
7/27/2007	**$511.89**	**$498.88**	**$30.53**	**$507.86**	**5.96%**	**Stopped Out at Circle B**	**5.30%**
8/3/2007	$503.00	$503.00	$30.00	$507.86	5.96%		
8/10/2007	$515.75	$502.50	$29.89	$513.50	5.80%		
8/17/2007	$500.04	$480.46	$28.85	$548.61	5.77%		
8/24/2007	$515.00	$496.00	$29.04	$545.30	5.64%		

Table 4.1 (Continued)

Week-Ending Close Date	Week-Ending Closing Price	Week's Lowest Low	Expected Move	Stop Loss	Percent of Price	Status	Net Profit
8/31/2007	$515.25	$505.79	$28.54	$545.30	5.54%		
9/7/2007	$519.35	$511.47	$28.45	$545.30	5.48%		
9/14/2007	$528.75	$510.88	$28.76	$528.74	5.44%		
9/21/2007	$560.10	$524.07	$27.81	$519.53	4.97%		
9/28/2007	**$567.27**	**$560.00**	**$28.60**	**$531.39**	**5.04%**	**Bought at Circle B**	
10/5/2007	$594.05	$569.61	$33.40	$536.20	5.62%		
10/12/2007	$637.39	$593.95	$38.13	$555.81	5.98%		
10/19/2007	$644.71	$611.99	$40.85	$571.14	6.34%		
10/26/2007	$674.60	$636.28	$41.20	$595.07	6.11%		
11/2/2007	$711.25	$672.09	$48.19	$623.89	6.78%		
11/9/2007	$663.97	$661.21	$49.00	$623.89	7.38%		
11/16/2007	**$633.63**	**$616.02**	**$46.76**	**$623.89**	**7.38%**	**Stopped Out at Circle C**	**10.00%**
11/23/2007	$676.70	$618.50	$49.94	$595.27	7.38%		
11/30/2007	$693.00	$650.26	$51.14	$599.11	7.38%		
12/7/2007	$714.87	$677.12	$52.75	$624.36	7.38%		
12/14/2007	$689.96	$681.21	$50.91	$630.29	7.38%		
12/21/2007	$696.69	$652.50	$51.41	$630.29	7.38%		
12/28/2007	$702.53	$693.06	$51.84	$641.21	7.38%		

Notice that for the entire year of 2007, this methodology recommended that you own shares of GOOG only twice. It recommended a buy in April and then stopped out in July for a net cash gain of 5.3 percent. Then, another buy was recommended in September and then stopped out in November for a net cash gain of 10 percent. For the 2007 year, these two investments would have generated you a net cash gain of 15.3 percent, and you would have had your cash exposed for a total of only six months. That is a net annual return of over 30 percent. Considering the broader market gained only 7.4 percent in 2007, this was a huge gain and 400 percent better than an average market index—and at far less risk since your investment was in the market for only six months.

What You Learned in This Rule

Rule 4 is the "Sell" rule. In this rule, you learned:

- Why it is important to remove market and data noise from your thinking.
- That selling is far more important than buying.
- How and when to sell.
- How to completely remove the emotion of trying to guess the right time to sell a long position or cover a short position.
- How to calculate an expected move for each stock in your portfolio so you know when that stock has begun to exhibit pricing action that signals a change in direction and a potential new trend that could significantly erode your hard-earned, but unrealized, gains.
- Why using a stop loss is an essential investment strategy.
- How to calculate that stop loss without emotion or stress.
- How to let your stop loss settings be your exit strategy for each of your stocks.
- Most importantly, how to sleep at night without worrying about your stocks and that you can go on vacation again without constantly watching stock prices.

Never Marry a Stock
(For Adults Only!)

*"Never love something (or someone) that can't love you back;
especially stocks!"*

$$\begin{array}{ccc} \text{Smart} & + & \text{No} & = & \text{Profitable} \\ \text{Trades} & & \text{Emotion} & & \text{Relationships} \end{array}$$

Let's review briefly. You've learned how to think like a fundamentalist, how to use Demand Fundamentals to select only the best stocks,
how to refine and narrow that "best list" of stocks by looking at relative value, how to time your entry point through the use of a simple
but profoundly powerful technical analysis, and how to know when
to sell through the use of an Intelligent Stop Loss® strategy.

In Rule 5, you will learn to remove emotion from owning stocks.
You will learn how to be agnostic about the holdings in your portfolio. Why do you suppose that so many investors (and this may very
well include you) have an ongoing love affair with one or more of
the stocks in their portfolio?

Don't get me wrong—love is a wonderful thing. You can love
your spouse, your children, your grandchildren, your home, your
work, your country, or even the stock market, like I do. You can love
the fact that you may have made a lot of money in the stock market.
But you should never, never love a stock.

More Love, Less Money

There is an old saying that "love is blind." There is a *lot* of truth to that statement. Love tends to gloss over the blemishes and highlight the faintest glimmer of anything positive. Ask any mother, and she will tell you she has the most beautiful children. Ask any grandparent, and they will tell you they have the most incredible, intelligent, witty, handsome, and beautiful grandbabies in the world. (Well, at least mine are.) This is human nature and something that is wonderfully special about human beings. Unfortunately, this is a terrible quality to have when it comes to owning stock.

Too many times, investors become foolishly infatuated with a stock or a sector (how about those gold bugs) or an entire market. These investors become almost childish in their complete abandonment of common sense as they let emotion take over their investment life. This phenomenon is not restricted by age or gender or race. It can happen to the most sage, wizened, and mature investors. When emotion takes over, mature judgment and reasoned investment strategies fall by the wayside.

As I have mentioned before, I get the opportunity to attend a number of investor-related events each year. During these events, I get into many different conversations with individual investors. Invariably, there will be someone who wants to know what I think about the current political machinations erupting from Washington, D.C. My wife, Sue, warns me before each of these investor meetings not to get into a political discussion with anyone. I try very hard to heed her advice. But, sometimes, an adept conversationalist will draw me into a discussion about why the current party in power is taking our country to "hell in a handbasket," and they want to make sure I agree with them.

This is kind of like asking a man if he has quit beating his wife. Regardless of his answer, he has made the wrong response. So it is with politics. Do I have a strong political opinion? Absolutely! Does that opinion change my investment methodology? Absolutely not! Nor should it change yours.

It doesn't matter what your political leaning is. It doesn't matter if your stock is helped or hurt by the current political climate. It doesn't matter if our current president is a genius or a buffoon. It doesn't matter if Congress is doing the right or the wrong thing. You should not let your political opinions make your emotions gain any control over your investment methodology. When that happens, you will start buying or selling based on emotions and not on a solid set of rules.

Likewise, it is a mistake for you to have an emotional opinion of a publicly traded company. You may have heard of a fairly famous and very successful stock market investor, Peter Lynch. One of his most famous investment strategies is to "invest in what you know." This, on the surface, seems to make a lot of sense, but in reality, it doesn't make any sense at all. You see, Mr. Lynch is like a lot of Wall Street professionals. They reason that the average, nonprofessional investor doesn't have time to learn complicated quantitative stock analysis methodologies and, as such, just can't compete with those of Mr. Lynch's ilk. Therefore, the poor nonprofessional investor must be relegated to investing in stocks of companies that the non-professional investor has some tangible experience with. You, the average nonprofessional investor must "invest in what you know" or else you are just guessing and really have no idea what you should or should not be buying in the way of stocks.

I submit to you that you can do far better with your stock investment dollars than most of the Wall Street "professionals" by depending on a solid set of investment rules, instead of an anec-dotal and emotionally charged relationship you might have with a company's goods or services.

To "buy what you know" infers that your opinion of a compa-ny's goods and/or services means that the entire market has your same opinion. Just as in politics, you should not extrapolate your emo-tional opinions onto the public at large or the investor market for a particular stock. It is the epitome of arrogance to think that your opinion of a company's goods and services is the same view of an entire market. Buying "what you know" infers that if you like a product, you should like the company that produces that product, and that you should, therefore, buy stock because of your emo-tional attachment to the company behind that stock.

The Peter Lynches of the world can assume that you, the lowly nonprofessional can never compete in the professional world of stock investing and must rely on your emotions to pick stocks, but they are wrong. In this day and age, you have *all* the requisite access to financial information to have a rules-based quantitative investment methodology that is *not* tied to emotions. You have the ability to cre-ate an investment strategy that can and will produce consistent and significant profits in the stock market, and do so without emotional attachments.

My point in all of this is that you must strive to eliminate emotions from your investment strategy, even when the Wall Street moguls tell you that emotional investing is the best you can do.

Another reason to keep emotion out of your investment methodology is that emotion ignores common sense. Without common sense guiding your investments, you might as well be tossing a coin to make buying and selling decisions. Emotional investing is the worst kind of investing. It is the same thing as blind investing.

Emotional trading will cause you to be influenced from past entanglements with the company, such as liking their products or the amount of money you have made with that company in the past, or even a negative experience you have had with that company in the past. You must be very careful to avoid letting emotions and/or historical experiences with a company overly influence your trading decisions. Buying, selling, shorting, or covering is a decision that should be based on the merits of the event itself. You should strive to ignore past investments, losses, or gains, in a stock. Treat every trade as if it is the first trade you have ever made and that you have no "baggage" to influence that decision. Every trade should be viewed from the perspective of what you hope to gain in the future from the trade, not what that trade does for your past.

Leaving the Past Behind

Let's pretend you bought 10,000 shares of AAPL for $200 per share. This would be a $2 million investment into AAPL stock. For most of us, putting $2 million dollars into a single stock would be considered a significant investment. But you don't care. You *love* the Apple Corporation. You love their products. You hate Microsoft and you *love* Apple. You love their user-friendly computers, their iPhone, their iPod, and all their other products. You believe that Steve Jobs is a giant among his peers. You could not be more proud of your $2 million dollar investment into Apple! Hopefully, by now, you can see how wrong it is to be investing in any company based on a love affair with the company, its products, or its management personnel. But, just to drive this point home, I am going to continue with the scenario.

Steve Jobs

Steve Jobs cofounded Apple Inc. In 1986, he acquired the computer graphics division of LucasFilm Ltd., which was spun off as Pixar Animation Studios. He remained its CEO and majority shareholder until its acquisition by the Walt Disney Company in 2006.

Now, let's say AAPL begins to move lower in price. Let's pretend it moves lower by 10 percent. If you were following Rule 4, the Stop Loss Rule, you would have likely already stopped out. At this writing, the stop loss for AAPL is about 8.19 percent below last week's lowest low. So, at a 10 percent pullback, you would have sold AAPL.

But you look at how much money you would lose if you sold and realize that would cost you a whopping $200,000. That's a *lot* of money. Plus, you still love Apple and you are convinced that the AAPL stock will soon recover. You didn't, after all, buy AAPL on a "trade; no, you "invested" $2 million dollars into Apple, the company. You're not going to give up on that investment for just 10 percent!

Then the AAPL stock moves down another 20 percent. You are now showing a paper loss of $600,000! You are not happy about the stock's market price and start thinking evil thoughts about those ignorant people out there that are pushing Apple's stock lower. They are all just a bunch of market manipulators and worse, particularly those scums, the short sellers of AAPL!

You can't possibly sell now. You have invested too much money into the AAPL position and cannot face the real loss of $600,000. So you hold on, hoping the stock will someday recover. It might— or it might go even lower. There were many people who thought the same thing about Enron[1] a few years ago.

If you had not had such a love affair with Apple and the impact of losing $200,000, you would have been out of AAPL with a loss of 8 percent or so. Now, you are facing a loss of more than 30 percent and still can't manage to get away from your emotional and financial tie to the AAPL stock.

---

[1]Before its bankruptcy in late 2001, Enron employed several thousand people and was one of the world's leading electricity, natural gas, pulp and paper, and communications companies. It reported revenues of $111 billion in 2000. *Fortune* named Enron "America's Most Innovative Company" for six consecutive years.

It is times like these when an investor quits thinking about cutting losses or preserving capital and blindly plunges forward, believing (or hoping) that only good things can happen in the future. They blindly marry into a stock or a company and are convinced the marriage will last forever. Unfortunately, reality will set in sooner or later. An old country music song had the following, paraphrased, lyrics: "I went to bed with a 10 and woke up with a 2!" This is a story that has more truth in it than many investors want to admit.

In the above example, you married and went to bed with a stock that represented the best technical company in the world—a "10." Now, down more than 30 percent and still dropping, you have come to realize that you woke up with a disaster—a "2." That's what happens when you marry a stock and fall in love with an inanimate object that can *never* love you back!

So . . . Are You Married to a Stock?

I like to say, "Never marry a stock because you won't like the divorce!"

Here are some ways you can tell if you are married to a stock, and what to do about it:

- *You love the dividend.* You bought this stock when it was selling for less than $2 and now it is trading at $60, and its dividend yield at current prices is 4 percent, but that equates to 120 percent due to your basis in the stock. You see no reason to ever sell this stock. Although there may be a very good reason to own a stock, it still does not justify taking the position of never wanting to sell. You are so in love with this stock that you are blinded by the relative yield. The fact that a company has paid a dividend for decades does not mean it will always pay a dividend. Plus, no company is totally immune from going out of business. Even with the scenario described above, you should seriously consider what it would take for you to sell that stock. Then, set your stop loss or exit strategy accordingly.
- *You love the products that the company makes.* You love their management style. You are a part of their culture (cult—i.e., you're drinking their Kool-Aid) and you feel proud to own shares in this company. You have seen this company struggle against far stronger and better-capitalized competitors, and

yet this company has prevailed. When you think about the shares of stock you hold in this company, you have a warm, glowing feeling about your commitment to them. You are definitely married to this stock!

The sad truth is that regardless of how much you love a company and its stock, that stock does *not* love you back. Companies are businesses, not emotional beings. The mandate of the company is to build shareholder value, and regardless of how you may think otherwise, the ultimate success or failure of the company is measured in return on equity. A company has no feelings. It has no emotion. Companies do not have souls. Companies are business entities run by human beings. This company does not care about your hopes and aspirations. It does not care that you are trying to provide for your family. When this company's board meets, they do not discuss how close you are to achieving your goals for retirement. They do not think about you in the least, other than as a minuscule statistical component of their millions of shareholders. You may love your stock in this company, but your love is definitely unrequited.

- *You did a lot of research on this company before buying its stock.* You were convinced your investment would pay off handsomely. After you invested a substantial amount of your life's savings into this company, its stock went higher and higher and higher still. You were so proud of your investment prowess. You bragged to your friends about how smart you were to buy in just when you did. Thinking about this investment made you smile. Then, the stock began to trade lower and lower and lower still. At one point, you had lost all your one-time profits and were down more than 30 percent. You couldn't stand it any longer. Your only hope was to cut your cost basis in half. You knew that if you doubled the number of shares you own, you could cut your 30 percent loss to just 15 percent. What did you do? You doubled the number of shares you had by buying more, with the hope that the stock would rebound enough for you to get out. But it didn't move higher. It moved even lower. You hate this stock. You wish you had never bought it. You want out, but you can't leave—you are married to this stock, so you hang on, hoping that one day it will recover to some of its glory days.

This is a tragic story that is repeated all too often by thousands of investors. You are emotionally tied to the fear of losing money and admitting that you made three terrible mistakes: You made the mistake of buying the stock; you made the mistake of not selling when it had gone up so much; and you made the mistake of buying more of such a loser. You are in a death spiral and don't know how to get out. Actually, this divorce is easier to resolve than most. Just ask yourself this question: If you had the cash instead of the shares, would you buy the stock now? If the answer is yes, then hold onto it. If the answer is no, then sell it. In either case, use Rule 4 to set your stop loss.

- *Many investors believe that if they own shares of stock in a company, they actually own part of the company.* This might be legally true, but it is completely false in practical application. Sure, if you own a huge percentage of a company's outstanding shares, you can have some influence with the company's management, but you still don't own the company. You don't actually own the assets of the company. You don't have any liability for their debts. You merely own a piece of paper that represents a small percentage of "control" of the company. But even if you own a lot of shares, you still can't control the company. Don't believe me? Here is a test for you that will prove it to you. The next time a company declares that it is going bankrupt, buy some shares of the company and see how much you get back when the company is liquidated. You will get nothing. The shareholder stock does not provide you with actual, physical ownership of any assets of the company. One hundred percent of the assets of the company belong to the company, not the shareholders. The only people who ever get anything back from a company that is liquidated are the creditors, and oftentimes, they don't get anything either. So, don't fool yourself into thinking that when you buy shares of stock, you are buying ownership in a company. You are not. You are only buying ownership in shares of stock. Those shares of stock only have value if there is a market for those shares. Otherwise, they are worth less than the paper they are printed on.

The simple implementation of Rule 5 is never to get married to a stock. Being emotionally attached to stocks will always lead you down the path of this pseudo-marriage. If a stock performs well, you will tend to like that stock more. The better it does, the more you like it. Soon, "like" turns into love, and suddenly you are married!

"Why," you may ask yourself, "is it so wrong to be married to a stock? After all, I have made a lot of money from this stock. I like the company. It has provided me with a lot of income. It is furnishing me a significant portion of my livelihood in my retirement. I like being married to this stock."

Here is why you should never be married to a stock.

No company is immune to the vagaries of the economy. As I have said before, any company, regardless of its size or longevity, can fall on hard times and can even go bankrupt. Being married to a company means you are using emotion instead of reason and logic to hold shares in the company. Emotion is an anathema to smart, intelligent investment strategies.

Regardless of how long you have held a stock and regardless of how low your basis and regardless of your current financial condition, you should have an exit strategy for every stock in your portfolio.

You should sit down right now and put a price (e.g., stop loss order) on every stock in your portfolio. Ask yourself this question: "Is there any price that would cause me to believe it is a good time to sell?" If you cannot come up with a price, then you are so emotionally tied to the stock that you are at risk of losing everything you have in that stock. This is because any stock, at any time, can suddenly become worthless. Don't believe me? Just recently, one of the largest banks in the world (Bear Stearns) went from being worth $160 per share to only $2 per share in a few months. Indeed, at the end, this same company went from being worth $50 per share to $2 per share in less than three days.

Don't let your emotions rule your stock investments. The risk is just too great that you could lose everything.

How to Avoid Falling in Love with a Stock

You do not have to let your emotions rule your investing methodology and strategy. There is a simple way to keep emotion out of your stock market activities. Here is how:

1. Develop a solid set of rules to follow for making stock market trading decisions. These 10 Essential Rules are an excellent set of rules that will work for any investor.

2. Don't violate your rules regardless of what your emotions tell you. Gut instinct is good, but it should be used to help you build your rules, not steer your stock selections.
3. Finally, keep this in the forefront of your mind when it comes to making consistent profits in the stock market: **Your *rules* should completely govern how you invest in the stock market, but *you* should completely govern your rules.** When it comes to the decision-making process for stock market investing, follow your rules zealously!

What You Learned in This Rule

In this "adults-only" rule, you learned:

- Why it is important to not let the past overly influence your trading decisions.
- How to know if you are married to a stock.
- Why it is wrong and can be devastatingly expensive to be married to a stock, especially when you are served divorce papers by your stock.
- How to avoid being married to a stock.
- That following a good set of rules will help you process through the emotions of owning a stock.

RULE

Follow Only "Some" Insider Trading

"Monitoring insider selling is a total waste of time!"

$$\begin{array}{ccccccc} \text{Strong} & & \text{Bottoming} & & \text{Insider} & & \text{Huge} \\ & + & & + & & = & \text{Upside} \\ \text{Fundamentals} & & \text{Technicals} & & \text{Buying} & & \text{Potential} \end{array}$$

By the time you get to this rule, you are well on your way to knowing how to find the best stocks to own, when to buy them, and when to sell them. You also know how to avoid getting emotionally attached to your stocks.

Now, it is time to start doing a little refining of your growing and evolving investment strategy. Let's move on to see what we can glean from insider trading.

In this rule, you will learn how to analyze legal insider trading and how to use the data to help you make a final, perhaps critical, decision on selecting and/or ranking the stocks that you may consider adding to your portfolio. Finding the right stock that fits all of your requirements for buying out of many thousands of stocks is truly akin to finding a needle in a haystack. We want to narrow that search down to just a handful of the best of the best. We will do that by using insider trading data, but we'll use only one very specific type of insider trading data.

What Is Insider Trading?

Insider trading is a term that most investors have heard and usually associate with illegal activities. But the term actually includes both legal and illegal conduct. The legal version is when corporate insiders—officers, directors, and employees—buy and sell stock in their own companies. When corporate insiders trade in their own securities, they must report their trades to the Securities and Exchange Commission (SEC). Illegal insider trading refers generally to buying or selling a security, in breach of a fiduciary duty or other relationship of trust and confidence, while in possession of significant nonpublic information about the security. Insider trading violations may also include "tipping" such information, securities trading by the person "tipped," and securities trading by those who misappropriate such information.

Insider trading is illegal only when a person bases his or her trade on information that is unavailable to the public. It is also illegal to give insider information to another person, whereby that person makes equity trades based on that information. There is very little illegal insider trading since those who practice it are so easily caught and almost always face significant fines and jail time. For example, Martha Stewart was convicted of lying to the SEC regarding insider trading information. She was told by her friend Sam Waksal that his company's (ImClone) cancer drug had been rejected by the Food and Drug Administration (FDA) before this information was made public. The rejection by the FDA was very damaging to the company and resulted in a dramatic drop in share price. However, Martha Stewart avoided this drop in share price because she sold her shares before the FDA news was made public.

Martha Stewart

Martha Stewart is an American business magnate, author, editor, and homemaking advocate. She is also a former stockbroker and fashion model. Stewart has held a prominent position in the American publishing industry as the author of several books and hundreds of articles on the domestic arts, editor of a national housekeeping magazine, host of two daytime television programs, and commercial spokeswoman for K-mart. In 2001 she was named the third most powerful woman in America by *Ladies Home Journal*. In 2004 she was convicted of lying to investigators about a stock sale and served five months in prison.

Samuel D. Waksal

Samuel D. Waksal founded the biopharmaceutical company ImClone Systems in 1984. He was arrested on June 12, 2002, on insider trading charges, and subsequently pleaded guilty to charges of securities fraud, bank fraud, obstruction of justice, and perjury.

Some Insider Trading Is Great News

On the legal side of insider trading, there are two trades that can occur: insider selling and insider buying. Let's just deal with the legal side. A lot of investors think that *insider selling* is important information to know.

When I speak to large audiences, while the room is filling up, I like to chat with the audience and get to know them a little better and to give the audience an opportunity to warm to my presentation style of speaking. A question that I often ask is, "Could I see a show of hands of everyone who believes it is important for investors to monitor insider selling?"

I am always surprised at how many hands go up, although each year there seems to be fewer and fewer, which is a good thing.

Many investors seem to think that if an insider is selling, it must be because the insider knows the company is doing poorly or will soon have problems. This is almost always *not* the case because if an insider sells on this information, that person is committing a felony. There are hundreds of reasons for insider selling. Here are just a few:

- The insider is required to exercise stock options and must sell stock to pay for the options.
- The insider needs money to pay for his/her children's college education.
- The insider needs to pay off major medical bills.
- The insider wants to diversify his/her portfolio and owns too much of the company's stock and, therefore, must sell shares.
- The insider owns too much of the company's stock and, due to the requirements of an upcoming merger, the insider is required to divest (sell) a significant portion of his/her shares in order for the merger to take place.

- The insider wants to buy a second home or pay off the mortgage on his/her first home.

In fact, more times than not, when insiders sell, it is likely that the company is doing well and will do well in the future. I know that sounds counterintuitive, so let me explain.

Because insider trading is so highly scrutinized by the SEC and because there is the potential for serious consequences regarding illegal trading, many corporate insiders wait until there is not even the hint of bad news on the horizon before selling shares. Insiders can be somewhat paranoid about selling shares at any time, since it is possible for bad news to come out later on the company. Even if they didn't know about the news in advance, they will likely be investigated and accused of trading on insider knowledge.

This is why many executives have a preset formula for selling shares so that they can rightly claim that the selling of shares was predetermined by formula and had nothing to do with insider knowledge.

So, with this in mind, my philosophy is to ignore insider selling.

However, there is only *one* reason for insider buying: The insider believes the stock in the company is cheap compared to where it should be. Insider buying can also be deemed illegal if the insider is buying stock based on information not available to the public. But insiders have the opportunity to look at the company from the inside out. No one is likely to know better about the health and future growth of the company than an insider. When an insider buys, it is almost always a very good indication that good things are more likely on the horizon for the company, rather than bad things.

How to Use Insider Buying Information

When you have several stocks that are otherwise equal in quality and opportunity for pricing growth and you are trying to decide which is the better stock to buy, always look at the insider buying.

Figure 6.1 shows an example chart of CHK (Chesapeake Energy Corporation). At the time of this writing, CHK was a Demand Fundamental buy-rated stock, according Rule 1. But at the same time CHK was buy-rated, there were more than 40 other stocks that were also buy-rated, among the 6,000 stocks that I track at any one time.

When I began narrowing down my list of stocks to buy, one of the major criteria that I consider is insider buying. I consider it a very big plus when a stock that I am considering to buy has a recent record of strong insider buying.

Take a look at Circle A in Figure 6.1. Notice how the significant increase in insider buying coincides with a low point in the stock's market price (Circle B). But what is so very important and often very typical is the directional move of the stock's pricing trend in the months that followed that strong level of insider buying. The stock went on a multimonth run, with the market price of shares moving nicely from the lower left to the upper right.

When you are looking to add a new position to your portfolio, you want as many positive, growth-oriented activities as possible supporting your trade. It is almost never a good idea to be a loner when it comes to buying stocks. It is far better to be in with the crowd that is pushing your stock's price higher and higher. So when you are trying to make a final decision on which stock, look at buying alongside the insiders.

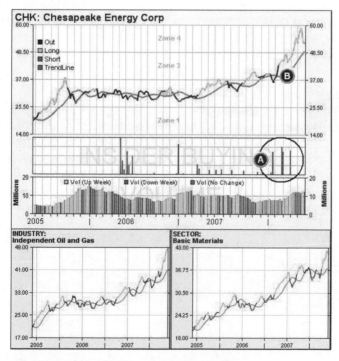

Figure 6.1 Chesapeake Energy Insider Buying

But as with the other rules in this book, do not use insider buying as the only criterion for buying a stock. When I am considering a new stock to buy, insider buying is one of the last things that I consider, not one of the first.

Look back at Figure 6.1. There are many reasons to buy this stock at Circle B, not the least of which is insider buying. The trading volume was increasing, which is a very good sign. The industry, independent oil and gas, was moving into bull mode, which was extremely positive and supported buying the stock. The sector, basic materials, was also moving into bull mode.

Every technical indicator was positive, including insider buying. With the Demand Fundamental supporting the trade and the technical supporting the trade, CHK was certainly one of those screaming buy situations at Circle B.

I hope you see how clearly you can arrive at a decision to buy or sell with this methodology. You don't have to read bulletin boards, analyst reviews, trade journals, and financial newsletters, or listen to talking heads on TV to know exactly when to buy and exactly when to sell with this methodology.

By this point, you should begin to see how you can take control of your stock market investment strategy and know exactly what to do in all markets and at all times!

What You Learned in This Rule

In this rule on insider trading, you learned:

- Why insider selling data is virtually irrelevant when considering whether to enter into or exit out of a stock holding.
- Why insider buying can provide great insight into the next several months of the performance of the stock's share price.
- That the first step in making consistent profits in the market requires making good stock selections from the entire universe of stocks. At any given time, there are likely to be dozens (sometimes hundreds) of stocks that have great fundamentals and great technicals and are efficiently priced—many more stocks than you could buy even if you wanted to. It is at times like these that you must have criteria for screening the best of the best from the group of potentially great trades. Sometimes, only insider buying data will give you that edge to make your final selection.

R U L E 7

Watch the Institutional Ownership

"Contrary to what you hear on TV every day, there are no undiscovered stocks, so quit looking for them!"

$$\text{Strong Fundamentals} + \text{Strong Technicals} + \text{Moderate Institutional Ownership} = \text{Odds of Successful Trade Increase}$$

In Rules 1 and 2, you learned how find the best stocks to buy. You learned how to pick the best time to buy or short in Rule 3. In Rule 4, you learned when to sell. In Rule 5, you mastered how to avoid emotional entanglements with stocks. Rule 6 showed you how to use insider buying, not insider selling, to help you refine your list of stocks under buying consideration.

Rule 7 is another stock selection refinement rule. Here, you will learn how to use institutional ownership as another important element for finding just the right stock to buy at the right time.

Think with me here for a moment. What if I told you that all the big name institutional investors were going to put the combined resources of all their corporate research staffs together to find the very best companies with the best management teams, the best products, the best growth plans, the best products in the pipeline, the most undervalued, and the highest likelihood that the stock price for these companies was the most likely to move significantly higher? And when they complete this monumental task of analysis, and after they have narrowed their list down to just the few that they really want to own, they are going to call you up and tell you which companies that they have selected?

Do you think you could use this kind of information?

Amazingly, this is exactly what large institutions have to do. They have to report to the public exactly what they own and whether they have recently bought or sold shares in each company that they have traded. It's the law, and it is information that is available to you for free.

But before I get into the details about how to make the most out of this information, let's see why this information is so valuable to us.

Don't Be Misled

Some TV personalities and so-called financial experts will tell you that if you just listen to them or if you just "do your homework," you will find that next big "undiscovered" company. They want you to believe that you can find the next Microsoft or Apple; or worse, they want you to believe that if you will just listen to them, they will tell you something that "Wall Street" hasn't found yet. Of course, they want you to believe that you can "get in on the ground floor" and buy shares now before the big know-it-all Wall Street types can figure it out.

This is simply delusional and silly, at best. At worst, it is just a big lie.

I hate to break it to you, but for individual investors, there just are no undiscovered companies. By the time we think we have found an undiscovered jewel that is going to skyrocket as soon as Wall Street finds the company, Wall Street has already vetted the company and either bought shares or passed on the stock.

Vetted

Evaluated for possible approval or acceptance.

As individual investors, we don't have the manpower to peruse through the voluminous amount of data it would require to gain such information before the big institutions can find these undiscovered companies.

Big institutional investors have rooms full of MBAs who have only one job in life—to find undiscovered companies. If they don't find those companies, those MBA grads are fired. Major institutional investors have the resources and time to seek out and analyze every publicly traded company. If they find a winner, they buy in. They take a "pass" on all the other companies that don't meet their criteria for growth and quality.

To think that Wall Street has somehow missed a company, or that somehow you, as an individual investor, can find an undiscovered company before the big institutional investors find that company, is just wrong thinking. If the staffs of major institutional investors somehow miss a real gem of a company, heads will roll. People will be fired. No, every company that is worth owning has already been vetted by one or more of the big players on Wall Street, regardless of what you may have heard otherwise.

The Problems of Being a Major Institution

I am going to ask you to step into the shoes of a portfolio manager of a major institution. Your job is to find ways to invest in the stock market the billions of dollars held by the institution. And your job is on the line if you screw this up!

What's more, you have to report to the public exactly how you invested this money each quarter, so it puts even more pressure on you to make sure you pick the right stocks.

The good news is that you have a very large budget for research staff. You can hire anyone you want and buy all the research data you want. So you hire yourself a bunch of new MBA graduates, give them access to all available corporate research, and on top of all of that, you put together a field staff that is required to make on-site visits to every company your research staff tell you is a potential candidate for your portfolio.

Now, keep in mind that you have several billions of dollars and, as such, you have to look everywhere possible for companies to invest in. You never have enough good companies for the amount of money you have, so you continually put pressure on your research staffs to make sure not a single company is missed. They must scrutinize all public companies.

And every few days, your boss and your boss's boss come in to see why you aren't making them higher returns. This is really a high-pressure job!

Don't Believe the Wall Street Titans

You know, the arrogance of big name Wall Street investors never ceases to amaze me, and it doesn't matter if they live in Omaha, Nebraska, or New York, New York. They all seem to look down their noses at individual investors and tell them with some veiled disdain that there is no way that you, the lowly individual investor, can compete with their big money, big staffs, and almost infinite knowledge of the market and financial investing.

Don't you believe them! You not only can compete with these titans, but when it comes to net total return, you can outperform most of them most of the time. Warren Buffett may be happy with an 8 percent return on billions of dollars, but your return can average more than twice that amount virtually every year!

These 10 rules will put you on a course to outperform these Wall Street "titans." One reason is that you don't have to invest millions or billions of dollars at a time. You can afford to own smaller chunks of stock, and you can be much quicker on your feet—meaning you can get in and out of a trade very quickly, without worrying about the size of the trade and amount of money that will have to change hands.

Plus, you have access to enough information to make very informed and unbiased decisions about which stocks you will buy and when you sell. It is very, very unlikely that Warren Buffett has or needs a stop loss strategy. He can't afford to make decisions that quickly, but you can. The big titans of Wall Street have access to huge quantities of information on every market and every company in the world. You don't have that data, but you do have the results of that data by watching what companies the big institutions select for investment. Having access to the end results of institutional trading is just another way you can play on the same field as the biggest investors in the world when it comes to buying and selling stocks of publicly traded companies.

You may not have a room full of MBA graduates doing research for you, but you certainly can get access to the end results of all that institutional research data. And you can put that knowledge to great use. You have everything you need. You just need to know how to tap into this knowledge. Let me show you how.

Institutional Ownership

Institutional ownership refers to the total number of shares of publicly traded companies that are held (owned) by large financial organizations, pension funds, or endowments.

How to Use Institutional Trading

If these big institutional investors are already doing the hard work of finding all the undiscovered companies—all the companies worth owing—how does an individual investor tap into all the knowledge and investment research data? And how much will it cost you to obtain that information? You might be thinking, "Oh, if I could just peek over the fence to see what they are getting ready to buy." Well, it may surprise you, but, indeed, you can do just that!

Here's the good news: **There is really only one piece of information you need to know from these big institutions, and that is the percentage of ownership that they have in publicly traded companies.**

If institutional investors find a great company, they buy shares in that company, and they have to report their ownership to the public.

Finding that information is wonderfully simple. It is available for free. All you have to do is get on Yahoo! or MSN or Google or any web site that provides stock market data and you can find the total number of institutional investors and the percentage of the outstanding shares they own for every publicly traded company.

Think of it this way: Remember when I asked you to pretend you are the portfolio manager of a big institution earlier in this rule? Imagine you have just arrived at work. You go to your corner office. Your secretary has your favorite coffee ready and your day's agenda. She has all the financial newspapers for you, but the most important report she has for you are the results from your research staff. They have worked around the clock to provide you with a list of companies you should consider buying.

You make your decision and place your stock orders.

Now, a few weeks later, you have to report to the world what you own and how many shares you own. That's when you and I can peek over the fence.

That's when we know the results of all that expensive research and more expensive research staff.

If the results of the data recommend increasing ownership in a publicly traded company, then these big institutions will be buying more shares. If the results are negative, they will not be buying, or will even divest themselves of shares.

Watching and tracking the trading habits of big institutions as they increase or decrease their ownership in publicly traded companies is an excellent way to use the resources of their research departments. It *is* like peeking over the fence!

You Can Not Only Look Over the Fence—You Can Hop Over It!

Charting institutional ownership is a very good way to see trends that you can use to your advantage. It is also a great way to visually and rapidly determine if the institutional ownership is too light or too strong. Figure 7.1 is an example of a chart that I have used to track institutional ownership for the XYZ Company.

There is, surprisingly, quite a bit of useful information in a chart like this. Let's see what it has to tell us.

Look at Q1-05. The vertical bar represents the total percentage of outstanding shares owned by large institutions. This means that of all the shares available on the open market for the XYZ Company, 20 percent are owned by large institutions. This is a very good sign that at least some institutions have vetted the XYZ Company and have come away believing the company is solid, from a fundamental perspective, and its share price is likely to be increasing in the near future.

You will also notice that there is a black line on the Figure 7.1 chart. This black line represents the number of big institutions who own shares of the XYZ Company. The more big institutions that buy shares in a company, the better—to a point (more on this later).

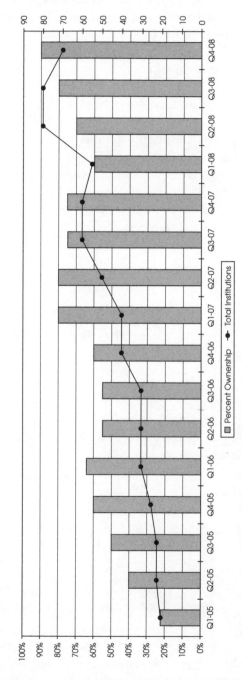

Figure 7.1 Institutional Ownership for the XYZ Company

You want to see, over time, that big institutions are buying more shares and that more institutions are buying into the company. Increasing institutional involvement in the company means that the word is spreading that the future is bright and growing brighter. Share prices should be increasing.

You can quickly see from a chart like the one in Figure 7.1 whether big institutions own any shares in the XYZ Company. With no vertical bars, the institutional ownership would be zero.

You can see if the XYZ Company stock is "under accumulation" if the vertical bars become taller from one quarter to the next. A stock that is being accumulated by large institutions is a very good indicator of future growth in the company. The institutions have analyzed the company and believe the company will grow, and, therefore, the share price will increase.

Under Accumulation

"Under accumulation" means that, over time, more shares are being purchased and held by the buyer. Generally, this is construed to be a very bullish indicator on the stock being accumulated, and it is likely that the stock's market share price will be increasing in the near future.

Likewise, if the stock is "under distribution," the vertical bars become shorter from one quarter to the next. A stock that is under distribution by large institutions means that the future growth of the company is not as strong as in the past. Institutions have analyzed the company and believe the company will grow, but not as fast as before, and the likelihood of the share price's increasing is not quite as strong as before.

Under Distribution

"Under Distribution" means that, over time, fewer shares are held by the holder as more and more shares are sold. Generally, this is construed to be a negative indicator on the stock, and it is likely that the stock's market share price will be decreasing in the near future.

If big institutions believe the company's stock will begin to move much lower because the future growth potential of the company is very negative, the institutions will bail out, often en masse.

A stock that is under distribution (being sold) is not a good sign if your goal is to be long in the stock. It is a great sign if you plan to short the stock. When a stock is under distribution, it means that large institutions have decided the company is overweighted in their portfolios and they are divesting (selling) shares.

Overweighted

Institutions have more of a particular company than they want to own.

Monitoring the total number of institutional owners is also a good indicator of future share price movement—the more institutional owners, the better, for upward pricing movement.

How to Interpret Institutional Ownership

When making a decision on which stock to buy or short, institutional ownership can provide you with some critically important insight. It is important to understand the impact of institutional ownership and whether that ownership helps or hurts your ability to generate a profit from the stock you are considering for purchase.

The following are some key elements to consider when analyzing institutional ownership:

- A company's having no institutional ownership is a negative indicator. This means that big institutions have analyzed the company and have decided to pass on any ownership. Major institutions have huge sums of money to invest, so they are always looking for good opportunities. If there is not significant institutional participation in a stock, then it is probably not the best stock selection for a long position. Another way to think about this is to recall our wildebeest herd analogy. In this case, the herd is the collective world of big institutions. If your stock is *not* in the middle of the herd and moving from lower left to upper right (in this case, the analogy would be "shares under accumulation"), then you should seriously consider not buying this stock. Keep in mind that I will, on occasion buy a stock that is not owned by any major institutions, but the Demand Fundamentals, the industry and sector charts, the directional move on average trading volume, and the stock's technical chart *must* be overwhelmingly compelling.

- One of the goals of big institutions is to do all they can to drive up share price in their portfolio companies. So, institutional ownership is a good thing when it comes to analyzing a potential addition to your portfolio. It is good to buy stocks that have institutional ownership. It is better to buy stocks that have an upward trend in the percentage ownership by institutional investors. You want to see shares under accumulation. Referring back to Figure 7.1, you want to see the vertical bars getting taller and taller. And you want to see the number of institutions holding shares in your stock increasing from one quarter to the next.

- There is a downside to institutional ownership when institutions own too many of the outstanding shares of a company. When institutions decide to sell or divest themselves of ownership in a company, they tend to sell very large numbers of shares. And it is not uncommon that when one institution starts selling, others will follow in rapid succession. This is the wildebeest herd. Remember, when they turn and start running in another direction, the whole herd turns. Soon, there can be a huge sell-off in a stock when nothing in particular has happened to the company. But, when this sell-off happens, the share price can plummet if institutions own too much of the company. For example, if institutions own 20 percent of the outstanding shares, the impact of a 5 percent sell-off by institutions is significant, but not overwhelming. However, if institutions own 98 percent of the outstanding shares, a 5 percent sell-off can have a huge impact on share price and can lead to a 10 percent or 20 percent reduction in share price, once the selling begins.

- I have found the following to be very good rules of thumb when it comes to institutional ownership:
  1. Consider it a negative if there is less than 5 percent institutional ownership in a company. This does not prohibit you

from buying shares in the company, but it is a negative that you should weigh when making your final stock selection. Buying a stock with less than 5 percent institutional ownership adds a little risk to your investment.

2. Consider it a negative if there is more than 95 percent institutional ownership in a company. Again, this does not prohibit you from buying shares in the company, but it is a big negative, especially if you eventually accumulate a lot of unrealized gain in your stock. An institutional bailout could wipe out your gains in a matter of seconds. So buying a stock with 95 percent or more institutional ownership adds quite a bit of risk to your investment.

3. Stocks that have between 30 percent and 60 percent institutional ownership are considered in my "sweet spot." These are stocks that have been seriously vetted by several big institutions and have impressed their research staffs sufficiently to cause some serious investment in their stocks by large institutions. At the same time, the big institutions do not own so much of the outstanding shares as to force a pricing collapse if they decide to sell.

What You Learned in This Rule

In this rule, you learned:

- Why watching large institutions buy and sell stock in publicly traded companies should be an important component of your investment strategy.
- That a good rule of thumb is to avoid stocks that have institutional ownership of less than 5 percent or more than 95 percent.
- **That the sweet spot for institutional ownership is 30 percent to 60 percent.**
- That it is very important to understand that Rule 7 is not to be taken as the only criterion for selecting a stock. It is just another of the 10 rules in this book that is intended to help you choose between two stocks that are, in all other ways, identical in fundamentals and technicals.

But, when you have to make a final selection from a very small group of stocks under your consideration, you should use institutional ownership as one way to make your final selection.

R U L E

Stay Diversified

"If you assume the worst is possible, you will never be surprised."

$$\begin{array}{c} \text{Balanced} \\ \text{Industries} \end{array} + \begin{array}{c} \text{Balanced} \\ \text{Sectors} \end{array} = \begin{array}{c} \text{Balanced} \\ \text{Lower Risk} \\ \text{Portfolio} \end{array}$$

At this point, you have learned how to use fundamentals and technicals to find the right stock at the right time to buy. You have learned how to set an exit strategy and not to get emotionally attached to a stock. You have learned how to use insider buying and institutional ownership to further refine your stock selection process.

But if all you do is find the right stocks to buy at the right time, you can still fail (and fail miserably) at building a world-class portfolio of stocks. Rules 8 and 9 will teach you how to balance your investments based on the amount of money you have to invest in the stock market and, at the same time, avoid putting too many of your eggs in one basket.

Rule 8 is all about diversification. In this rule, you will learn how proper diversification can save your investment life when all else fails.

Do Not Put All Your Eggs in One Basket

You have heard all your life that you shouldn't put all your eggs in one basket. In other words, you should not put your entire life's financial security into a single investment or single type of investment. The reason is obvious, of course. The risk is just too high that something unforeseen could happen and either financially cripple you or, worse, wipe you out completely.

I doubt there are very many investors who do not clearly recognize the truth in that saying. But you might be surprised at how few investors do much more than pay lip service to this axiom of life.

It amazes me how most investors either do not know how to stay diversified or they simply believe the worst cannot happen to them. I was at a meeting recently where I was extolling the importance of a sensible, rules-based approach to diversification. From the back of the room, a gentleman raised his hand and said that well-diversified portfolios couldn't make enough profit for him. He went on to say that he purposely keeps his portfolio undiversified.

I'll admit that his remarks surprised me. I'm sure a lot of investors may think that, but it is rare to hear someone actually proclaim it as a strategy.

My response to him was that I place too high a value on low risk and that I am quite satisfied to make 20 percent or more per year with highly diversified portfolios. I could tell from his body language that he was skeptical. I wasn't sure if his skepticism was about the 20 percent or the risk comment.

It is possible that you can be lucky and bet the farm on a single strategy that pays off in huge returns. But do you really want to "bet the farm" when the "farm" is your entire financial life? I don't know of anyone willing to put everything at risk on one spin of the roulette wheel. Because that is exactly what it is—gambling. A poorly diversified portfolio is virtually the same as a turning your portfolio into a game of chance.

Stock market investing is *not* gambling if you are a rules-based investor and follow a regimented and disciplined investment strategy. However, if you guess at what to buy and when to sell and ignore diversification, you would likely be just as well off to go to Vegas and hit the gambling tables.

Smart diversification can turn your investments into money-making strategies. Lack of diversification will turn your investments into a game of chance.

Let me illustrate what I mean with a personal story.

Several years ago, when I only had 3 or 4 of my 10 rules in place, I was investing heavily in the stock market. It just so happened that real estate investment trusts (REITs) were doing extremely well. In fact, they were doing so well that you could hardly lose money if you invested in REITs. In many ways, it was kind of like printing money. It didn't really matter which REIT you bought; it would move higher in price. Several of the REITs hadn't issued a sell signal for more than two years!

REIT

A real estate investment trust that purchases and manages property and/or mortgage loans. REITs are traded just like stocks.

I began buying more and more REITs. It wasn't long before REITs made up more than 60 percent of my portfolio. It wasn't uncommon to make more than 6 percent and sometimes more than 10 percent gains in my entire portfolio on a weekly basis. I would give a huge excited whoop every time I looked at my portfolio! I was a genius! There was no doubt that I was becoming one of the most successful stock market investors to have ever lived! My name would soon be in lights!

I was bragging about my stock market prowess to one of my investor friends who had been investing in the market for decades before I began investing. He asked me, "What percent of your total portfolio is devoted to REITs?"

I said, "60 percent and I'm thinking about adding more!"

He said, "Don't you think you are a little overweighted in REITs?"

I told him, "Absolutely not. I've got many different types of REITs, including rental property, commercial property, mortgages, land, malls, and so on. I am extremely diversified. And besides, it doesn't really matter. I've got stop loss settings on all my REITs, so if something bad happens, I'll be more than okay. In the meantime, I want to keep this thing going!"

Well (some of you already know this next part, because perhaps you experienced it, too), it was only about a month later that the bottom fell out of the REIT industry. Some REITs lost more than 40 percent within a matter of hours. I lost more than 20 percent of my portfolio's value in just a few days' time. I saw more than eight months of growth in my portfolio's value lost—in less than two weeks.

I had no excuse. It was my ego, arrogance, greed, and stupidity that put my financial net worth at serious risk. That was an extremely valuable lesson to learn. Why is it that it seems the best lessons learned are almost always the most expensive?

I learned more than one lesson in that REIT debacle. I learned that unrealized gain is a fleeting mistress that looks real in one moment and vaporizes in the next. I learned that older, wiser investors should be carefully and respectfully listened to. I learned that the less diversified my portfolio, the more risk is in my portfolio. I also learned that regardless of how successful you are in the stock market, the market has a very bad habit of knocking you down when you least expect it. I learned to hope for the best, but plan for the worst—always!

How to Be Diversified

Of course, to be properly diversified, you must first understand what it means to be diversified. Owning three different types of REITs is *not* diversification.

Diversification

A portfolio strategy designed to reduce exposure to risk by not putting too much of the portfolio's value in any one type or group of stocks, which could all move negatively in the same direction. The ultimate goal of diversification is to reduce or mitigate risk of loss in a portfolio. Risk becomes mitigated by the fact that not all stocks will move up and down in value at the same time or at the same rate. Diversification reduces both the upside and downside potential and allows for more consistent profits over a wide range of markets.

Assuming you read the definition of diversification, your objective is to not own too many stocks that belong to the same group. You remember, of course, our beloved wildebeest. In this case, think of the herd as an entire sector of stocks, where each Wildebeest is a different stock. Now, let's assume the herd is merrily romping across the savanna when a pride of lions lunges out of the tall grass right in the path of the herd. In a heartbeat, the whole herd suddenly changes from romping to running hard and moves quickly in the opposite direction. If all your stocks were in that herd, you could go from gaining share price to suddenly losing share price and in a big way.

Staying with that analogy, you can think of industries as small herds of stocks. Sectors are large herds of stocks. In either case, you do not want to have all of your stocks in a single herd. A good approach to diversification would be to keep a reasonable limit of stocks in each different industry and different sector. That way, you could be reasonably assured that the lions would not attack all herds at the same time from the same direction. In this way, you have lessened your risk to significant loss.

Industry

A category of business activity that describes a very precise business activity (e.g., semiconductors or shipping). This categorization of stocks is based on each company's major source of revenue, competitors, products, markets served, and so on. Every stock belongs to only one industry designation. Every industry belongs to only one sector designation.

Moving away from the wildebeest analogy, diversification is nothing more than making sure you don't have too much of your money tied up in too few sectors and industries. Since every stock belongs to an industry and a sector, the simplest way to maintain reasonable diversification is to control the percentage of your portfolio by sector and industry.

Sector

A group of similar Industries. A sector can be a group of one or several industries. An industry is a group of one or several stocks.

Currently, there are about 11 sectors and over 250 industries. Every stock belongs to one and only one sector and one and only one industry. Every industry belongs to one and only one sector. Some sectors have dozens of industries and several hundred stocks. Some sectors have only a couple industries and very few stocks. Some industries have many stocks and some have only a few.

It is not important that you know how many stocks are in each sector and industry as much as you know that sectors are comprised of groups of industries and industries are comprised of groups of stocks.

In this way, you can quantify how much of your portfolio is devoted, by percentage, to sectors and industries.

Following is a series of lists[1] of the 11 major sectors. Below each sector is a list of industries associated with or belonging to the sector.

I show you this list to make sure you understand the granularity of the groupings. Too many times, you hear a comment from a financial pundit stating something about the Energy sector or the Oil sector or the Precious Metals sector. None of those terms are correct. There is no such designation as "Energy sector." There is a "Basic Materials" sector that has a lot of energy-related stocks in various industries, such as Oil and Gas operations, but nowhere is there a designation of "Energy." All this means that various organizations arbitrarily assign a different classification to various groups of stocks. It doesn't matter which nomenclature you use as long as you use the classification to help you stay diversified in your portfolio.

As for this list of sectors and industries, I am totally agnostic. It matters not a bit to me which of these sectors or industries or the stocks contained therein that I select for my portfolios, and I strongly suggest you remain just as agnostic. What matters is whether the stock selected meets your requirements for quality, as defined in Rules 1, 2, 6, and 7; that the stock meets your requirements for the right time to buy as defined in Rules 3 and 10; and that the stock stays within your diversification requirements as defined in Rules 8 and 9.

Following this list, you will learn how to set the limits of how much of your portfolio can be allocated to sectors and industries.

---

[1] The sector and industry naming convention is the standard designation provided by Interactive Data Corporation.

Industries in the Basic Materials Sector

The Basic Materials sector is a group of industries that are involved with the discovery, development, and processing of raw materials. The industries in the Basic Materials sector are:

- Agricultural Chemicals
- Aluminum
- Chemical Manufacturing
- Chemicals—Major Diversified
- Chemicals—Plastics and Rubber
- Coal
- Copper
- Gold and Silver
- Gold Industry
- Independent Oil and Gas
- Industrial Metals and Minerals
- Iron and Steel
- Major Integrated Oil and Gas
- Metal Mining
- Miscellaneous Fabricated Products
- Nonmetallic Mineral Mining
- Oil and Gas—Integrated
- Oil and Gas Drilling and Exploration
- Oil and Gas Drilling and Exploration
- Oil and Gas Equipment and Services
- Oil and Gas Operations
- Oil and Gas Pipelines
- Oil and Gas Refining and Marketing
- Oil Well Services and Equipment
- Paper and Paper Products
- Silver
- Specialty Chemicals
- Steel and Iron
- Synthetics

Industries in the Capital Goods Sector

The Capital Goods sector is a relatively small group of industries that are related to the manufacture or distribution of goods. There is a small number of industries, but those industries contain a diverse set of companies. The industries in the Capital Goods sector are:

- Aerospace and Defense
- Construction—Supplies and Fixtures
- Construction Services
- Miscellaneous Capital Goods

Industries in the Consumer Cyclical Sector

The Consumer Cyclical sector is a group of consumer-related industries that are sensitive to business cycles, whose performance is strongly tied to the overall economy. Consumer Cyclical companies tend to make products or provide services that are in lower demand during economic downturns and higher demand during economic upswings. Following is a list of industries in the Consumer Cyclical sector:

- Apparel—Accessories
- Audio and Video Equipment
- Auto and Truck Manufacturers
- Auto and Truck Parts
- Furniture and Fixtures
- Jewelry and Silverware
- Photography
- Recreational Products

Industries in the Consumer Goods Sector

The Consumer Goods sector includes a wide range of industries' products, from clothing and footwear to household and personal products. Within this diverse sector are the following industries.

- Appliances
- Auto Manufacturers—Major
- Auto Parts
- Beverages—Brewers
- Beverages—Soft Drinks
- Beverages—Wineries and Distillers
- Business Equipment

- Cigarettes
- Cleaning Products
- Confectioners
- Dairy Products
- Electronic Equipment
- Farm Products
- Food—Major Diversified
- Home Furnishings and Fixtures
- Housewares and Accessories
- Meat Products
- Office Supplies
- Packaging and Containers
- Personal Products
- Photographic Equipment and Supplies
- Processed and Packaged Goods
- Recreational Goods, Other
- Recreational Vehicles
- Rubber and Plastics
- Sporting Goods
- Textile—Apparel Clothing
- Textile—Apparel Footwear and Accessories
- Tobacco Products, Other
- Toys and Games
- Trucks and Other Vehicles

Industries in the Consumer Non-Cyclical sector

The Consumer Non-Cyclical sector is a group of consumer-related industries that are not sensitive to business cycles, whose performance is not strongly tied to the overall economy. Consumer Non-Cyclical companies tend to make products or provide services that are consistently in demand during all economic fluctuations. Following is a list of industries in the Consumer Non-Cyclical sector:

- Beverages (Alcoholic)
- Beverages (Nonalcoholic)
- Crops
- Food Processing
- Personal and Household Products

Industries in the Financial Sector

The Financial sector is a group of industries that comprise financial institutions and financial markets. It has often been said that the Financial sector leads the economy into and out of recessions. The following industries are included in the Financial sector:

- Accident and Health Insurance
- Asset Management
- Closed-End Fund—Debt
- Closed-End Fund—Equity
- Closed-End Fund—Foreign
- Consumer Financial Services
- Credit Services
- Diversified Investments
- Foreign Money Center Banks
- Foreign Regional Banks
- Insurance (Accident and Health)
- Insurance (Life)
- Insurance (Property and Casualty)
- Insurance Brokers
- Investment Brokerage—National
- Investment Brokerage—Regional
- Investment Services
- Life Insurance
- Miscellaneous Financial Services
- Money Center Banks
- Mortgage Investment
- Property and Casualty Insurance
- Property Management
- Real Estate Development
- Regional—Mid-Atlantic Banks
- Regional—Midwest Banks
- Regional—Northeast Banks
- Regional—Pacific Banks
- Regional—Southeast Banks
- Regional—Southwest Banks
- Regional Banks
- REIT—Diversified

- REIT—Healthcare Facilities
- REIT—Hotel-Motel
- REIT—Industrial
- REIT—Office
- REIT—Residential
- REIT—Retail
- S&Ls—Savings Banks
- Surety and Title Insurance

Industries in the Health Care Sector

The Health Care sector is comprised of a group of industries that focus on medical and health care goods or services. Stocks in the Health Care sector are frequently considered to be defensive because the products and services are essential. This means that even during economic downturns, people will still require medical aid and medicine to overcome illness. This consistent demand for goods and services makes this sector less sensitive to business cycle fluctuations. The industries in the Health Care sector are:

- Biotechnology
- Biotechnology and Drugs
- Diagnostic Substances
- Drug Delivery
- Drug Manufacturers—Major
- Drug Manufacturers—Other
- Drug-Related Products
- Drugs—Generic
- Health Care Plans
- Health Care Facilities
- Home Health Care
- Hospitals
- Long-Term Care Facilities
- Medical Appliances and Equipment
- Medical Equipment and Supplies
- Medical Instruments and Supplies
- Medical Laboratories and Research
- Medical Practitioners
- Specialized Health Services

Industries in the Industrial Goods Sector

The Industrial Goods sector is comprised of a group of industries that focus on machinery, manufacturing plants, materials, and other goods or component parts for use or consumption by other industries or firms. Generally, when demand for Consumer Goods increases, the demand for Industrial Goods also increases. The industries in the Industrial Goods sector are:

- Aerospace-Defense—Major Diversified
- Aerospace-Defense—Products and Services
- Cement
- Diversified Machinery
- Farm and Construction Machinery
- General Building Materials
- General Contractors
- Heavy Construction
- Industrial Electrical Equipment
- Industrial Equipment and Components
- Lumber, Wood Production
- Machine Tools and Accessories
- Manufactured Housing
- Metal Fabrication
- Pollution and Treatment Controls
- Residential Construction
- Small Tools and Accessories
- Textile Industrial
- Waste Management

Industries in the Services Sector

The Services sector is a group of industries that provide intangible products (services) that are not goods (tangible products) to consumers. Industries included in the Services sector are:

- Advertising
- Advertising Agencies
- Air Delivery and Freight Services
- Air Services, Other
- Apparel Stores
- Auto Dealerships

- Auto Parts Stores
- Auto Parts Wholesale
- Basic Materials Wholesale
- Broadcasting—Radio
- Broadcasting—TV
- Broadcasting and Cable TV
- Building Materials Wholesale
- Business Services
- Casinos and Gaming
- Catalog and Mail Order Houses
- CATV Systems
- Communications Services
- Computers Wholesale
- Consumer Services
- Department Stores
- Discount, Variety Stores
- Drug Stores
- Drugs Wholesale
- Education and Training Services
- Electronics Stores
- Electronics Wholesale
- Entertainment—Diversified
- Food Wholesale
- Gaming Activities
- General Entertainment
- Grocery Stores
- Home Furnishing Stores
- Home Improvement Stores
- Hotels and Motels
- Industrial Equipment Wholesale
- Jewelry Stores
- Lodging
- Major Airlines
- Management Services
- Marketing Services
- Medical Equipment Wholesale
- Movie Production, Theaters
- Music and Video Stores
- Personal Services
- Printing and Publishing

- Publishing—Books
- Publishing—Newspapers
- Publishing—Periodicals
- Railroads
- Real Estate Operations
- Recreational Activities
- Regional Airlines
- Rental and Leasing Services
- Research Services
- Resorts and Casinos
- Restaurants
- Retail—Apparel
- Retail—Catalog and Mail Order
- Retail—Department and Discount
- Retail—Home Improvement
- Retail—Specialty
- Retail—Technology
- Schools
- Security and Protection Services
- Shipping
- Specialty Eateries
- Specialty Retail, Other
- Sporting Activities
- Sporting Goods Stores
- Staffing and Outsourcing Services
- Technical Services
- Toy and Hobby Stores
- Trucking
- Wholesale, Other

Industries in the Technology Sector

The Technology sector is a comprised of a group of industries that focus on the application of information in the design, production, and utilization of goods and services, and in the organization of human activities. Industries belonging in the Technology sector are:

- Application Software
- Business Software and Services
- Communication Equipment
- Computer-Based Systems

- Computer Hardware
- Computer Networks
- Computer Peripherals
- Computer Services
- Computer Storage Devices
- Data Storage Devices
- Diversified Communication Services
- Diversified Computer Systems
- Diversified Electronics
- Electronic Instruments and Controls
- Healthcare Information Services
- Information and Delivery Services
- Information Technology Services
- Internet Information Providers
- Internet Service Providers
- Internet Software and Services
- Long Distance Carriers
- Multimedia and Graphics Software
- Networking and Communication Devices
- Personal Computers
- Printed Circuit Boards
- Processing Systems and Products
- Scientific and Technical Instruments
- Security Software and Services
- Semiconductor—Broad Line
- Semiconductor—Integrated Circuits
- Semiconductor—Specialized
- Semiconductor Equipment and Materials
- Semiconductor—Memory Chips
- Semiconductors
- Software and Programming
- Technical and System Software
- Telecom Services—Domestic
- Telecom Services—Foreign
- Wireless Communications

Industries in the Transportation Sector

The Transportation sector is comprised of a group of industries that focus on transporting people and/or goods from one physical location to another.

- Miscellaneous Transportation
- Water Transportation

Industries in the Utilities Sector

The Utilities sector is comprised of a group of industries that focus on utilities such as gas and power. The Utilities sector typically performs best when interest rates are falling or remain low. The industries included in the Utilities sector are:

- Diversified Utilities
- Electric Utilities
- Foreign Utilities
- Gas Utilities
- Natural Gas Utilities
- Water Utilities

A little later in this rule, you will see an example portfolio that is well diversified by sector and industry. Remember, from an agnostic point of view—the view I want you to have—it doesn't matter which stock or which industry or which sector. The right stock within the right industry and the right sector will be determined through your application of Rules 1, 2, 3, 6, 7, and 10. Once you have selected the stocks you are considering to buy, you will use Rules 8 and 9 to see if you have sufficient room, on a percentage basis, to add those stocks to your portfolio.

If you already have too much of your portfolio invested in a certain sector or industry, you will have to bypass adding another stock in that sector or industry to your portfolio, *regardless* of how much you want to buy the stock and *regardless* of how great the stock looks from your application of these 10 Rules in your analysis of the stock.

So just how do you determine if you can add a great stock to your portfolio? The answer is all about how you enforce diversification in your portfolio.

How to Enforce Diversification

The wonderful part about following the diversification rule is that it allows you to add further distance between your investment decisions and your emotions. As I have said before, emotions are an anathema to your ability to make money in the stock market.

As I alluded to in my story on failing to heed a strong diversification strategy at the beginning of this rule, markets tend to move up or down in large groups of stocks. Right now, commodity stocks are universally surging higher almost every day, while the homebuilder stocks have plummeted to decade lows.

You could buy stocks that focus on gold, oil, wheat, silver, gas, corn—it doesn't matter. If it is a commodity stock, it is going higher. And there are dozens of stocks from which to choose. It would be easy to load your portfolio up with stocks that would make you a lot of money, but if or when those stocks quit moving higher, they most likely won't be sending you a message telling you to sell at the top. Odds are, you will get caught in a big pullback in these stocks as the big institutions unload them in order to capture profits. When that time comes—and come it will—you won't be able to get out of those stocks fast enough. If they occupy too large of a position in your portfolio, you could easily lose a significant portion of your net worth.

So it is important to have some kind of control or limit on how many stocks of a certain type you can or should have in your portfolio at any one time, regardless of how strong those stocks might be with regard to share price appreciation.

Like everything else in this book, I have a formula for diversification that should be zealously followed, and this rule is no exception.

The Diversification Rule: Do not invest more than 30 percent of the total *value* of your portfolio in any one sector and no more than 20 percent of the total *value* of your portfolio in any one industry.

As simple as this rule is, it is profoundly helpful as you build, manage, and grow your portfolio of stocks. Often, you will find several great stocks you want to have in your portfolio, and if you were not following this rule, you could easily find yourself significantly overweighted in one sector or industry.

Staying diversified will keep you out of trouble. It will keep you from letting greed manage your portfolio instead of commonsense rules. Table 8.1 is an example portfolio that will help illustrate how to implement this rule.

The column entitled "Pct by Basis" is the percentage of the portfolio used to buy each of the 10 positions. You should note that the approximate distribution is about 10 percent (there will be more on this in Rule 9). The assumption is that the portfolio started out with $30,000 to invest in the market.

Table 8.1 Example Portfolio

	Shares	Basis per Share	Total Basis	Pct by Basis	Current Price	Total Value	Pct by Value
GNA	240	12.90	3,096.00	10.32%	14.99	3,597.60	11.99%
AGU	40	65.10	2,604.00	8.68%	73.77	2,950.80	9.84%
APA	30	107.01	3,210.30	10.70%	114.71	3,441.30	11.47%
NEU	50	61.18	3,059.00	10.20%	66.95	3,347.50	11.16%
RNST	140	21.47	3,005.80	10.02%	21.06	2,948.40	9.83%
WMT	60	49.78	2,986.80	9.96%	49.59	2,975.40	9.92%
BVN	100	32.50	3,250.00	10.83%	76.30	7,630.00	25.43%
DVN	40	74.13	2,965.20	9.88%	102.72	4,108.80	13.70%
ECA	50	58.98	2,949.00	9.83%	76.21	3,810.50	12.70%
GGB	200	14.22	2,844.00	9.48%	32.77	6,554.00	21.85%
Total Percent				**99.90%**			**137.88%**

The total percent of the portfolio, from a basis perspective, is 99.90 percent. This means virtually the entire portfolio is invested.

The column entitled "Pct by Value" represents how much of the original $30,000 is held by each position. Some positions have lost some money; others have gained. The total percent of the portfolio, based on the current share price (lower right corner) is 137.88 percent. This means the portfolio has a profit of 37.88 percent.

Just by looking at the list of stocks in the table and the percentages, would you say this portfolio is appropriately diversified? You will find out whether it is diversified as we work our way through the analysis of the portfolio.

Now, let's look at the same example, but include a column for industry and see how much of the *basis investment* of the portfolio is devoted to each industry (see Table 8.2).

Remember the rule: no more than 20 percent in any one industry.

Figure 8.1 shows a pie chart of the portfolio by industry, using the *original basis investment*. It is a graphic representation of the Total Basis column from Table 8.2. You should note that this portfolio is overweighted in the Independent Oil and Gas industry. The maximum allowable is 20 percent. In this example, the total amount invested is 30.42 percent, which is 10.42 percent over the limit.

There are three stocks listed as having Independent Oil and Gas as the associated industry: APA, DVN, and ECA. The Oil and Gas industry is overweighted in the portfolio by more than a third. The maximum amount of the portfolio that should be allocated to one industry is 20 percent. Something has to be done to correct this overweight situation. There are two choices:

1. Sell enough shares of each of the three holdings in that industry (APA, DVN, ECA) to get it down to 20 percent.
2. Sell all of one of the holdings.

Either way, other than adding more money to the portfolio, the total number of shares held in this industry has to be reduced.

Table 8.2 Example Portfolio—Industry View

Ticker	Industry	Shares	Basis per Share	Total Basis	Pct by Basis	Current Price	Total Value	Pct by Value
GNA	Steel and Iron	240	12.90	3,096.00	10.32%	14.99	3,597.60	11.99%
AGU	Agricultural Chemicals	40	65.10	2,604.00	8.68%	73.77	2,950.80	9.84%
APA	Independent Oil and Gas	30	107.01	3,210.30	10.70%	114.71	3,441.30	11.47%
NEU	Specialty Chemicals	50	61.18	3,059.00	10.20%	66.95	3,347.50	11.16%
RNST	Regional—Southeast Banks	140	21.47	3,005.80	10.02%	21.06	2,948.40	9.83%
WMT	Discount, Variety Stores	60	49.78	2,986.80	9.96%	49.59	2,975.40	9.92%
BVN	Gold Industry	100	32.50	3,250.00	10.83%	76.30	7,630.00	25.43%
DVN	Independent Oil and Gas	40	74.13	2,965.20	9.88%	102.72	4,108.80	13.70%
ECA	Independent Oil and Gas	50	58.98	2,949.00	9.83%	76.21	3,810.50	12.70%
GGB	Steel and Iron	200	14.22	2,844.00	9.48%	32.77	6,554.00	21.85%
Total Percent					**99.90%**			**137.88%**

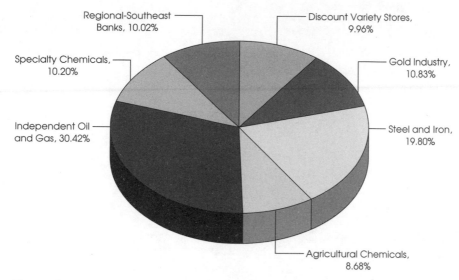

Figure 8.1   Portfolio Diversification by Industry (Original Basis)

Determining Industry Distribution

Now let's look at the same industry distribution, but instead of looking at what we paid for the stocks, let's look at the industry distribution based on each stock's *current value.* Figure 8.2 shows the value distribution represented in the Total Value column derived from the example portfolio shown in Table 8.2.

Hopefully, you can see that this portfolio is in even more trouble with regard to diversification. Independent Oil and Gas is still 8 percent overweight, and the Steel and Iron industry has jumped from about 20 percent to nearly 25 percent, which is 5 percent overweight.

The fact that the portfolio is growing is a good thing—it is, after all, what we want to have happen. But this growth has added a *lot* more risk to the portfolio by concentrating too much of your net worth in these two industries. A sudden downward change in investor sentiment in either of these industries could cost you a lot of lost profit. One of your goals is to gain and retain profits. This portfolio is now so badly diversified that you can only hope to get it back under control before something catastrophic happens in the market.

What do you do to fix this? The answer is simple: Just sell enough shares to get the total value of the portfolio by industry down to or below 20 percent per industry. What do you do with the cash generated from the sale of shares? Keep the cash in the

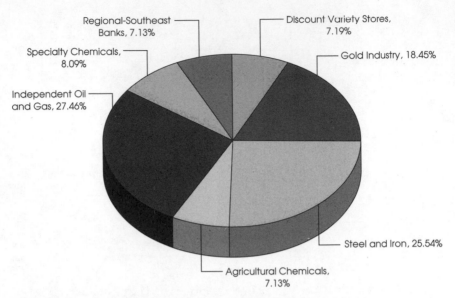

Figure 8.2   Portfolio Diversification by Industry (Current Value)

portfolio for the time being or, if you can find suitable stocks in other industries, consider adding those stocks to the portfolio. **Regardless of your actions, do not let any industry occupy more than 20 percent of your portfolio.**

Determining Sector Distribution

Now, let's turn our attention to the sector distribution. Take a look at Table 8.3, which is the same portfolio, but now you can see how the sectors are represented.

If you thought this portfolio needed work from an industry perspective, I hope you can readily see that there is a very serious problem in Table 8.3. Just look at how many positions are represented by the same sector: Basic Materials. The complete lack of diversification is obvious, but look at Figure 8.3 to really put this in perspective.

Nearly 80 percent of the *basis in the portfolio* (the amount you originally invested) is devoted to just one sector. This portfolio is extremely at risk of a potential market correction and a resulting huge loss in your net worth. It is critically important that this portfolio be rebuilt to where no more than 30 percent of the portfolio is devoted to any one sector.

Table 8.3 Example Portfolio—Sector View

Ticker	Sector	Shares	Basis per Share	Total Basis	Pct by Basis	Current Price	Total Value	Pct by Value
GNA	Basic Materials	750	12.90	3,096.00	10.32%	14.99	3,597.60	11.99%
AGU	Basic Materials	40	65.10	2,604.00	8.68%	73.77	2,950.80	9.84%
APA	Basic Materials	30	107.01	3,210.30	10.70%	114.71	3,441.30	11.47%
NEU	Basic Materials	50	61.18	3,059.00	10.20%	66.95	3,347.50	11.16%
RNST	Financial	140	21.47	3,005.80	10.02%	21.06	2,948.40	9.83%
WMT	Services	60	49.78	2,986.80	9.96%	49.59	2,975.40	9.92%
BVN	Basic Materials	100	32.50	3,250.00	10.83%	76.30	7,630.00	25.43%
DVN	Basic Materials	40	74.13	2,965.20	9.88%	102.72	4,108.80	13.70%
ECA	Basic Materials	50	58.98	2,949.00	9.83%	76.21	3,810.50	12.70%
GGB	Basic Materials	200	14.22	2,844.00	9.48%	32.77	6,554.00	21.85%
Total Percent					**99.90%**			**137.88%**

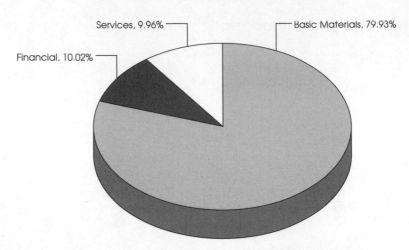

Figure 8.3   Portfolio Diversification by Sector (Original Basis)

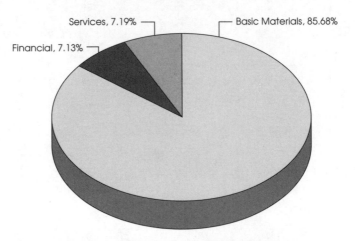

Figure 8.4   Portfolio Diversification by Sector (Current Value)

The distribution using the *current value of all positions in the portfolio* paints an even worse picture (see Figure 8.4).

What is the solution? Sell. Sell enough shares in the Basic Materials sector to bring the portfolio's commitment to Basic Materials to 30 percent or less. This may require that you sell out of some positions. This will also generate a significant amount of cash that you can use to buy other stocks. **But in no case should any one sector occupy more than 30 percent of the total value of your portfolio.**

The Right Diversification Strategy

The charts in Figures 8.5 and 8.6 are more in line with a good diversification strategy. In a 10-position portfolio, an industry chart should look like Figure 8.5.

The sector distribution chart should look more like Figure 8.6.

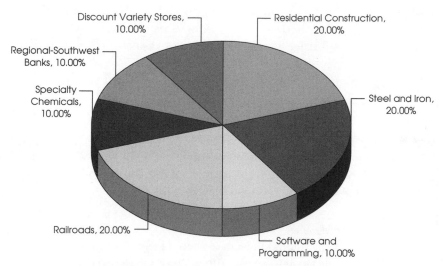

Figure 8.5   Appropriate Portfolio Industry Distribution

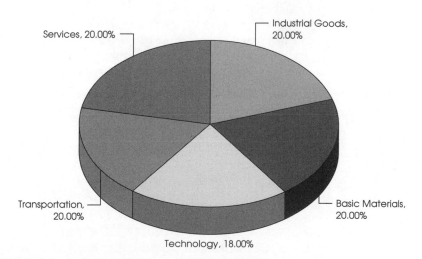

Figure 8.6   Appropriate Sector Distribution

This means that when you are looking for that next stock to add to your portfolio, you must first check *the percentage distribution* of the *current value* of the portfolio by industry and by sector.

I hope this rule has prompted you to take a few minutes and actually examine the stocks in your portfolio. Perhaps you even went so far as to build a pie chart to see where your distribution of stocks actually falls. I am thinking that some of you are a little surprised at how your pie chart is divided. You may be saying to yourself right now, "Good grief! I need to make some adjustments." It will be more comforting to you once you have your stocks in a more even distribution. You will definitely sleep better at night.

I zealously stay diversified, and I sleep very well at night!

What You Learned in This Rule

Rule 8 is a portfolio management rule that shows you how to keep your portfolio properly diversified. In this rule, you learned:

- Why diversification is important and what can happen if your portfolio is not well diversified.
- How to evaluate your portfolio to see how it is currently diversified by calculating the amount of the portfolio that is devoted to each sector and each industry.
- The maximum amount of your portfolio that should be concentrated in any one sector and any one industry.
- To consider both the basis you have in your portfolio by sector and industry, but more importantly, consider the current value of your holdings by sector and industry.
- How to get your current portfolio into proper diversification by selling shares in overweighted industries and sectors.

RULE

9

Balance Your Risk through Smart Asset Allocation

"The market loves teaching expensive lessons to overconfident investors."

$$\text{Total Investable Dollars} \div \text{Maximum Number of Positions in Portfolio} = \text{Perfect Balance}$$

Rule 9 is a companion rule to Rule 8. Where Rule 8 covered how to keep your portfolio diversified from a sector and industry perspective, Rule 9 covers a problem many investors have, which is how many stocks to own at any one time and how much money should be invested in each position.

Rule 9 is an amazingly simple rule, but it is extremely important for portfolio management. As a reminder, your goal is to build a world-class portfolio of stocks that will make consistent and significant profits in the stock market.

But making consistent profits in the stock market is more than just picking the right stock at the right time and/or selling the right stock at the right time. It also is about minimizing risk.

How Can I Minimize Risk While Making Profits?

Risk can be defined in many ways, but one element of risk which can and must be avoided is overweighting your stock investments by either having too few positions or putting more money into one position than you put into another.

You see, regardless of how adamant you are with your rules or how closely you stick to my 10 Essential Rules, the market will, on occasion, completely move against you and your best picks. There is no way to avoid this. It will happen just as sure as you are reading this book. One of these days, your best stock pick will turn out to be a real loser. It will completely defy all your rules and all your logic. It will move precipitously against you when you least expect it. Count on it. This will happen to you sooner or later. It happens to every stock market investor.

So, the best way to avoid this reversal of fortune is to never have too much of your net worth tied up in any one position. That way, even if that stock suddenly goes to zero, your total portfolio will not be significantly damaged.

This rule will give you the method and the formula for picking the right size portfolio, in terms of capital and number of positions to have in your portfolio, and it will give you the methodology for keeping your portfolio properly allocated with your investment dollars.

Rules 8 and 9 are like kissing cousins—closely related, if you will. They are easy concepts, and once implemented they function more like an insurance policy for your portfolio than anything else. Everyone understands the need for insurance: insurance for your home, your health, your car, your life, and so on. Why do you have insurance? It is to cover the cost of an event that could significantly impact your financial stability or the financial stability of others whom you want to protect. There are many reasons to have insurance, but all those reasons boil down to one desire or outcome: to provide enough cash to offset a major loss.

Rules 8 and 9 do not pay out cash, but these two rules will tend to do almost the same thing, they will mitigate your losses when the market moves against you.

But, here's an important fact. You can follow Rule 8 to the letter and still have your portfolio out of balance and, as a consequence, holding far too much risk.

You see, Rule 8 takes care of balancing your portfolio from a diversification perspective, but Rule 9 takes care of balancing your portfolio from an asset allocation perspective. If you recall, I explained in Rule 8 how to avoid putting too many eggs in one basket by not letting your portfolio become overweighted in any one industry or sector.

But, just as important as Rule 8 is for diversification, Rule 9 keeps you from having too much of your net worth tied up in any single stock. Always assume one of your stocks can go to zero before the market opens tomorrow. What would you do if your largest holding were to suddenly declare bankruptcy overnight and your stock's share price were to drop from $100 to $0 before the market opens the next morning? You haven't even had your first cup of coffee or turned on *Squawk Box,* a morning business news TV program! Impossible? Not hardly. It happens with enough regularity that you should be somewhat paranoid about this rule. It happened to Bear Stearns in less than 24 hours. Enron took longer, but it still left thousands of investors with $0 in value.

It is important—critically important—to do all you can to mitigate the risk of one of your stock holdings suddenly and catastrophically dropping in price. This kind of event can and will happen to you at some point in your investment life. It will happen when you least expect it. And it will hurt!

Therefore, you must always assume there is the possibility that any stock in your portfolio can suddenly and without warning plummet in price. This is why we use stop losses (Rule 4). But stop loss orders will do you no good if a stock's price drops from $100 to nearly $0. No one will be buying your stock and a stop loss order will be worthless. This is why we practice industry and sector diversification (Rule 8).

And this is why you must implement Rule 9.

Keep Your Portfolio Equally Weighted

Keeping your portfolio equally weighted means that if you have 20 positions in your portfolio, you should have no more than 5 percent of the *value* of your portfolio in each position. If you have 10 positions, you should have no more than 10 percent in each position. If you have 50 positions in your portfolio, you should have no more than 2 percent in each position.

The calculation is extremely simple: Decide how many stocks you are going to have in your portfolio and then divide that number into 100. For a 50-position portfolio, you divide 100 by 50, which is 2; which means no more than 2 percent of your portfolio should be held by any one position.

So, the next big question should be: How many stocks should you have in your portfolio? Following are some guidelines that will help you make that determination.

- **The amount of cash you plan to invest in the market matters.** The amount of money you plan to put to work in the market may constrain the number of positions you can have in your portfolio. This number is different for every investor. Determining this number can be nontrivial and should include an analysis of your financial condition, goals and objectives.

    As a general rule, however, if you have less than $5,000 to invest in the market, you would be wise to just select a broad index fund, or an exchange-traded fund (ETF), and not do a lot of trading. If you have less than $5,000 to put into the market, you should not be trying to build a portfolio of stocks. The primary reason is that in order for you to have a 20-position portfolio, for example, you could not invest more than $250 in each position. Some stocks cost more than $250 per share. But that's not the main reason. The main reason is every time you buy or sell a stock, your broker is going to charge you a transaction fee. Let's assume that fee is only $5. That means every time you make a trade, it is costing you 0.1 percent. It becomes very expensive if you are making several trades a month. Assume you make just 10 trades a month. That amounts to 1 percent per month in broker fees. Multiply that by 12 and those trades are costing you 12 percent per year. This means you have to make more than 12 percent per year just to break even. That is just too high of a hurdle for you to overcome.

    In a $10,000 portfolio, it is very difficult to achieve significant annual gains if you make very many trades in a year. In the above example, a $10,000 portfolio will spend 6 percent per year in trading fees. A $20,000 portfolio is getting far more reasonable. At $20,000, the above scenario results in only a 3 percent annual cost rate for trading fees. At $40,000, that 3 percent is down to only 1.5 percent; and so on.

The more money you can assign to your portfolio for stock trades, the lower your net cost of trades will be and the smaller that cost will be with regard to your net total return.

- **Determine your time management.** Next, you need to think about the amount of time you have available for the research, charting, and formula calculations. Maybe you have lots of time available for this effort. Maybe you have a day job. Maybe you have very limited time. If you follow my 10 Rules for consistent profits in the stock market, you will need at least one hour per week per position in your portfolio.
- **Have enough stocks to be properly diversified.** As a general rule of thumb, it is very difficult to be adequately diversified with fewer than 10 positions in your portfolio. However, a 20-position or 30-position portfolio can maintain excellent levels of diversification, especially if you include a few ETFs.

ETF

Similar to an index mutual fund, exchange-traded funds (ETFs) are designed to track different indexes, such as the Russell 2000 Index or the S&P 500 Index, or a particular industrial sector such as utility or bio-technology stocks. ETFs are different than index funds and sector funds because they are legally structured as stocks and are traded on stock exchanges just like any other stock and can be traded intraday and also sold short.

Figures 9.1 and 9.2 illustrate this concept a bit more graphically. Figure 9.1 represents a perfect value distribution of a 10-position portfolio, assuming it is 100 percent invested.

Current Value of the Portfolio

Determined by multiplying the number of shares by the current price of those shares, by position held.

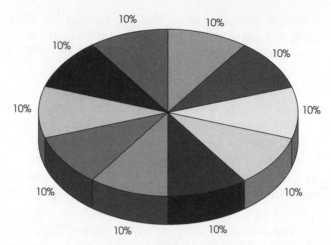

Figure 9.1   Portfolio Asset Allocation by Stock (100 Percent Invested)

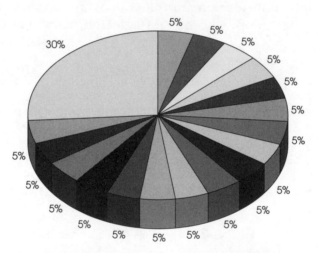

Figure 9.2   Portfolio Asset Allocation by Stock (70 Percent Invested)

Figure 9.2 represents a perfect value distribution of a 20-position portfolio with 30 percent of the portfolio in cash:

Rule 9 is all about allocating funds in your portfolio. *Keeping an even distribution is the key element mastering this rule.* To accomplish this task:

1. Decide on the total amount of money (cash plus total value of any stocks you own) you are going to devote to your stock

portfolio. As your portfolio grows in value, use the net total value of your portfolio for your distribution calculation.

2. Pick the exact number of positions you plan to have in your portfolio assuming you have 100 percent of your cash invested.

3. Divide the total value of your portfolio (cash plus value of equities) by the total number of positions you will have in your portfolio when fully invested. The result of this calculation is the maximum amount of cash you should devote to any one position. If you hold a position that is significantly higher than this amount, you might consider selling enough shares to bring it into compliance.

4. Keep your positions exactly at an even distribution. This does not mean you should be continually buying a few shares or selling a few shares just for the sake of balancing. Remember, each trade costs you a trading fee and you want to keep those fees to a minimum. Therefore, a good rule of thumb is to make adjustments only when a position gets more than 30 percent over its ideal distribution level. For example: Assume you have a 10-position portfolio and you bought a stock using 10 percent of the value of your portfolio. A little later down the road, that stock moves higher in price to where it is now occupying 13 percent of your total portfolio (that would be a 30 percent profit in that one position). At that time, you should consider selling enough shares to bring the total value of the position back to 10 percent of your total portfolio, remembering, of course, that your portfolio has grown in total value.

This math may seem a bit obtuse, but if you list your portfolio tickers, the number of shares, the basis for each position, and the current price, you can use a simple Excel worksheet to calculate the totals and percentages, making this process relatively easy.

What You Learned in This Rule

Remember, balancing your risk pays off in the long run, like a good insurance policy. Since there is no real insurance policy available for investing in the stock market (aside from using options, which is not covered in this book), we are obligated to implement one for ourselves, by keeping your investment risks to a minimum.

(continued)

In this rule, you learned:

- That diversification by industry and sector is not enough insurance against a catastrophic corporate failure.
- To never invest more money in one stock than you do in another. This doesn't have to be exact, but it should be within a 10th of a percent one way or the other from an equal distribution amount.
- To readjust the asset allocation in your portfolio when one of your holdings gets disproportionately overweighted due to increasing share price.

RULE
10

Make a Lot More Money by Timing the Market

"You have been told that you cannot time the market—you have been told wrong."

Stock		Sector		Industry		Market		Fully
Technical	+	Technical	+	Technical	+	Technical	=	Timed
Trend		Trend		Trend		Trend		Market

Okay, this is your final rule. This is the rule that ties everything together and moves you to being a master stock market investor. To become a master stock market investor, you must learn how to time the market. Very few stock market investors know how to achieve the goal of actually and consistently timing the market and timing it correctly. Follow the steps in this rule and you will know exactly how to time the market.

This rule will make timing the market a reality for you and, more importantly, show you how to make money when almost everyone else is losing money.

In this rule, you will learn how to master the art of knowing the best time to *buy* stocks, the best time to sell stocks and/or tighten your stop loss orders, and the best time to *short* stocks.

Hopefully, you have read and studied the previous nine rules and are ready to start building your world-class portfolio of stocks.

But is right now the best time to be buying stocks?[1] Maybe we are in a cyclical bear market; maybe we are topping out on a secular bull market; maybe we are facing a recession; maybe we are just coming out of a recession; maybe commodity stocks are soaring; maybe the dollar is plummeting; maybe a new war is about to break out; maybe interest rates are rising; maybe forecasters are predicting a market collapse; maybe we are in the middle of the biggest bull market in history or the worst bear market. Should you buy great stocks in a bear market? Should you buy stocks that are at lifetime highest highs in a bull market?

This rule is all about the timing aspect of buying and selling stocks.

The fact that you have found a great stock with super Demand Fundamentals and, seemingly, the ideal technical trend does not necessarily mean that you should buy that stock right now, in this particular market.

What is fascinating about this rule is that it will improve your ability to make consistent profits in the stock market, regardless of the methodology or trading strategy that you use. It doesn't matter if you are a day trader, an options trader, a swing trader, a momentum investor, or a market timer—this rule will make you more money and help you make smarter investment decisions.

Day Trader

Any individual who buys and sells the same security in the same trading day at least four times in a five-day period, and for whom same-day trades make up at least 6 percent of the trader's activity during that period.

Options Trader

Someone who buys and sells contracts that give the purchaser the right to buy or sell a security at a fixed price within a specific period of time.

---

[1]Remember, you can go to www.10EssentialRules.com to see what I am buying right now and what I have in my "10 Must Follow Rules" portfolio.

Swing Trader

An individual who makes short-term trades where a stock's price movement is in one direction; swing trading is a type of trading strategy that attempts to create profits by holding intraday positions for short lengths of time.

Momentum Investor

Someone who buys stocks or other securities that have had high returns over the past 3 to 12 months, and sells those that have had poor returns over the same period.

Market Timer

Someone who buys and sells equities using a strategy that is based on predicting market and economic trends, with the goal of anticipating future trends.

Why Having a Long-Term Investment Horizon Is Wrong

Financial advisers who tell you to have a 3-year, or 5-year, or 10-year investment horizon are only telling you this because they do not have a clue about how to time the market and, therefore, hope the market will continue higher if you just wait long enough. I would never pay someone for that kind of advice, and I hope you won't either. The main reason they want you to have a long-term investment horizon is that they hope you will forget the advice they gave you 3, 5, or 10 years ago.

You may be asking: Just how long should my investment horizon be to properly take advantage of the typical market swings? The answer is: just as long as the stock you are holding continues to make you more and more unrealized gains. When it stops making you a profit, you should sell it. Remember, you can always buy it again at a later date. My average hold time for stocks varies with the type of market we are in. At this writing, it usually ranges from 30 to 60 days.

There are times to be long in the market, there are times to be short in the market, and there are times to be out of the market. Without timing the market, you will sometimes be lucky, but most of the time you will be unlucky. Not all market timing strategies are good strategies. I use one in conjunction with my other nine rules, and not solely by itself. The one you will learn in this rule is an excellent market timing strategy, and it will serve you well all of your investment life.

Let me define for our use in Rule 10 the terms *Market* and *Timing:*

- *Market* refers to any of the following:
  - Broad indexes such as the S&P 500, the Dow 30, the Nasdaq, Global Markets, country exchanges (known as ETFs), and so on.
  - Sectors, including Basic Materials, Capital Goods, Financial, Health Care, and so on.
  - Industries, including Aerospace, Agriculture, Auto Manufacturers, Biotechnology, Business Services, Coal, Department Stores, and so on.
- *Timing* means picking a point in time in which it is more likely that future events will unfold in some predictable manner. If the market (as defined above) is exhibiting a downward trend, then the assumption is that the downward trend is bad for long positions in the market and good for short positions. Likewise, if a position in your portfolio has a sizable amount of unrealized gain and you have a normal stop loss order in place that, if triggered, would cause you to lose a substantial portion of that profit, knowing the market is about to reverse on you, it probably would be a great time to move your stop loss up and/or sell, thus capturing all or most of your unrealized gain and turning it into realized profit.

First of all, I want you to understand how to use timing data to help you manage your portfolio of stocks. I am going to take you through the charts[2] that you will need to use every week before making a single trade.

---

[2]You can find current updates to these charts at www.10EssentialRules.com.

There are five timing charts that come into play when deciding how and when to invest in the market. These charts are:

1. Historical Dow chart
2. Total Market Forecast
3. Weekly Bull/Bear Forecast
4. Sector chart
5. Industry chart

These charts will tell you not only the right time to buy, but whether you should be in or out of the market, and if you are in the market, whether you should have a bullish view or a bearish view of the near term.

Don't forget this very important concept: The best way to consistently make significant profits in the stock market is to buy the right stock at the right time and to sell that stock at the right time.

Timing is everything. Without a great timing strategy, you may as well have a buy-and-hope strategy.

Okay, let's get started with our first market timing chart.

The Historical Market Chart as Defined by the Dow

Figure 10.1 is a semilog of the Dow over the past 100+ years.

You may be familiar with this chart or you may have never seen it. It is a great chart that provides an excellent "big-picture" view of the total market. Now, before you get too worked up about my

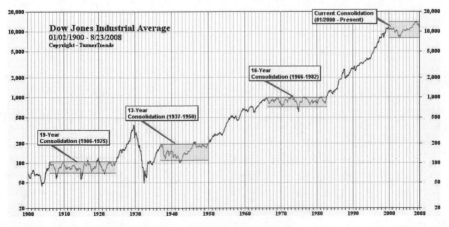

Figure 10.1   Historical View of the Total Market

using the Dow as opposed to the S&P 500 or some other larger cross-section, keep this in mind: The Dow has a typical correlation to the S&P 500 of over 95 percent. You can argue about minor details with regard to whether the Dow adequately and appropriately represents the overall market, but from a big-picture perspective, it does a marvelous job of tracking bull and bear markets and consolidation periods.

Consolidation Period

A period of time, generally of more than five years, where the market (in this case, the Dow 30) trades between a well-defined high and a well-defined low. The most recent consolidation, as of this writing, was between January 2000 and October 2006, where the Dow traded between a low of 8,000 and a high of 11,722.

From 1900 through 2007, there were four consolidation periods where the Dow traded in relatively narrow ranges:

- First consolidation (1906–1925): The Dow traded between 70 and 105.
- Second consolidation (1937–1950): The Dow traded between 110 and 195.
- Third consolidation (1966–1982): The Dow traded between 720 and 1,000.
- Fourth consolidation (2000–2008+): The Dow traded between 8,000 and 14,000.

When we are in a consolidation period, as we are as of this writing, an investor has a pretty good idea when to become very concerned about a market top and a market bottom. Figure 10.2 is an expanded chart of the fourth consolidation.

Once the Dow reached 14,000 and then retreated, an upper resistance level was set. This means it is likely that the Dow will, indeed, trade between a high of 14,280 and a low of 8,000 for 12 years or more, if it stays consistent with the previous three consolidation periods.

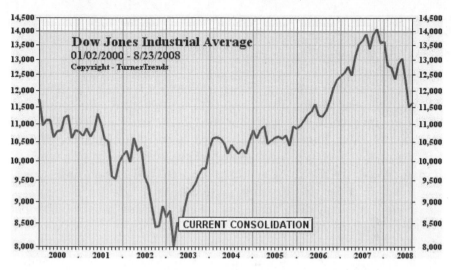

Figure 10.2   Most Recent Consolidation

You may be asking: Why is this important?

As a stock market investor, you should want to know if the market is going to trade in a range. That way, if the trend is moving lower within a consolidation period, you can decide either to be in cash or have a long or a short bias on the market. As the Dow gets closer to a resistance or support level, you can adjust your investment strategy and stop loss strategy accordingly.

Short Bias

When your opinion of the market is that it will go lower and, therefore, you will be either shorting stocks or buying inverse ETFs, or you will be in cash.

In Figure 10.2, the Dow is moving lower toward the middle of the current consolidation range. As an investor, there are two strategies that should be at play at this time:

1. Assume the market could be moving to 8,000, so there will be significant shortline opportunities.

2. Assume the market could reverse back toward the 14,000 resistance level. This means the market could move higher, but unlikely to move above 14,000.

It is amazing to me that when you listen to the talking heads on TV and read the financial press, most pundits seem to be confused about the market. Very few are looking at the market with a century view of the Dow. The Dow has been very consistent with its trends when in a consolidation period and when it breaks out of a consolidation period. When these trends are identified, it behooves investors to adjust their investment strategies accordingly.

If you knew nothing else about the market, these historical charts of the Dow would provide you with a very clear market bias; that is, whether to be buying or selling. But there is a *lot* more that the market can tell you about timing your investments for buying, selling, shorting and covering. Whereas the Dow helps us make big-picture decisions that have decade-long strategies, there are often smaller (cyclical) bull and bear market trends that occur inside consolidation periods and outside consolidation periods. This is where the Total Market Forecast comes into the picture.

The Market Trend and Correction Forecast

Markets move in both secular (more than a year) and cyclical (less than a year) cycles. Often, the talking heads like to refer to "Market Corrections," when the market sells off by 10 percent or more.

No one likes to be caught in a market correction when you want your investments to move in one direction, but the market is moving in the opposite direction and taking your stocks with it. Wouldn't it be great if you could avoid Market Corrections? Wouldn't it be great if you could sell your long positions just when the market is beginning to move much lower? Figure 10.3, the Market Trend and Correction Forecast chart, will go a long way in helping you avoid future market corrections. The algorithms in this chart and the forecasting component are registered with the U.S. Patent Office.

Market Correction

Occurs when the market drops (corrects) by 10 percent or more in a time frame of not more than two to three months.

Note the five black arrows in Figure 10.3. Each of those arrows is pointing to an early warning indicator to an impending market correction. This is an incredible chart for helping you time when to get in and out of the market. It provides a snapshot of the entire market. The data represented on this chart are the technical results of all the stocks that make up my total universe of stocks, which are most of the larger stocks traded on U.S. exchanges. These "technical signals" are exactly the same signals that you learned in Rule 3. There are two lines on this chart, representing the following:

- The total number of new technical short sell signals.
- The difference between the total number of new technical buy signals and the total number of new technical short sell signals.

Unlike the Dow chart, which is a century chart, the Market Trend Forecast chart is a much shorter and more recent time frame of the market, but the information that it provides is incredibly valuable.

In Figure 10.4, you see three letters, representing three previous market corrections or sell-offs.

Prior to these corrections, right after the composite line moved above and then back below the new short sell signals line, I was able to adjust my trading strategy such that I was able to avoid the corrections that has always occurred right after these crossing events. I would stop buying new positions and start raising my stops tighter

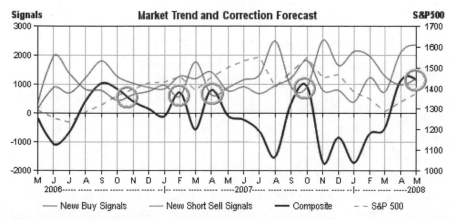

Figure 10.3   Market Trend and Correction Forecast

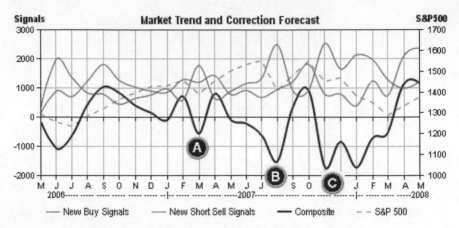

Figure 10.4   Previous Market Corrections

and tighter against the market price of my stocks. In 2007, using this methodology allowed me to generate more than a 30 percent gain in my portfolio.

Take a look at Figure 10.5, which is similar to Figure 10.4, but has some directional arrows added to it. The arrows provide a trading bias. If the arrow is sloping upward, the bias is bullish. If the arrow is sloping downward, the trading bias is bearish.

When the arrows slope upward, look for buying opportunities. When the arrows slope downward, look for short selling opportunities and/or move to cash by raising your stop loss orders. Don't forget that when the arrows slope downward, you can also look for opportunities to buy inverse ETFs.

Refer back to Figure 10.3 and take note of the peaks of the black, composite, line. When the black line (composite) moves above and then back below the new short sell signals line, it is indicative of a market top. At market tops, you want to be taking unrealized gains and moving those paper profits to real profits by looking for opportunities to sell. What is fascinating about this chart is that at these specific moments in time, the market is booming. Lots and lots of stocks are in bull mode with share prices rocketing upward. But when the composite line goes above and then starts to move back below the new short sell line, it means, almost certainly, that a correction is imminent.

When you think about it, this phenomenon makes sense. Market tops are always marked by surging upward prices with more

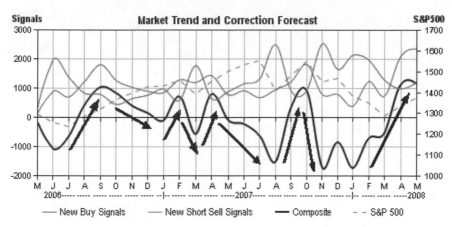

Figure 10.5 Buy/Sell Bias

and more new technical buy signals and a very small number of new technical short sell signals. You will notice the dropping number of short sell signals, just before a market top.

The Market Trend and Correction Forecast chart has accurately predicted every market correction since its inception back in 2006.

Think about it. You can avoid most, if not all, market corrections forever with this strategy!

How to Trade for Free (Almost)

Okay, we've gone from a century (the Dow chart) to a two-year (the Market Trend and Correction Forecast charts) to our next chart, the Bull/Bear Rating for the upcoming week. To generate this forecast, you need to apply Rule 3 to your universe of stocks. Then, compare the total number of new technical buy signals to the total number of new technical short sell signals for the most recent week-ending close.

From these two numbers, you can generate a ratio. For example, if you found that there were 250 new buy signals and 500 new short sell signals, the ratio would be 250-to-500; which is a ratio of 1-to-2. This means that for every new buy signal, there are two new short sell signals. This is a very bearish indicator and means that there is more money being taken out of the market than being put into the market, since selling tends to drive prices lower and selling takes money out of the market.

Lowering prices means more stocks are triggering new short sell signals. The more money that investors take out of the market, the more bearish the market becomes.

Likewise, the opposite would be true if the number of new buy signals was significantly greater than the number of new short sell signals.

I like to rank these ratios from a rating of −5 to a + 5, where −5 is extremely bearish and a rating of +5 is extremely bullish, as follows:

- 7-to-1 or greater is a – 5 rating when there are more new short sell signals than new buy signals.
- 7-to-1 or greater is a + 5 rating when the number of new buy signals is larger than the number of new short sell signals.
- 5-to-1 up to 7-to-1 is either a + 4 or a − 4, depending on which number represents the new buy signals or new short sell signals.
- 3-to-1 up to 5-to-1 is either a + 3 or a − 3, depending on which number represents the new buy signals or new short sell signals.
- 2-to-1 up to 3-to-1 is either a + 2 or a − 2, depending on which number represents the new buy signals or new short sell signals.
- 1-to-1 is neutral and generates a 0 rating.

Of course, the big question in your mind should be: What do I do with this Bull/Bear Rating? Primarily, you will use this rating to trade for free—meaning you can "effectively" avoid paying sales commissions to your broker. Let me show you how.

In Rule 4, you learned how to calculate the "expected move" (EM). This is the amount a stock can move against you and still be in an up trend. Another way to look at the EM is the amount the stock can fluctuate in price and still be within one standard deviation of its mean price.

One way to avoid the net negative impact of broker fees is to buy stocks for less than market price. You can avoid, in most instances, paying market for a stock by using limit orders that are set below market. The problem most investors have is how to set a limit order that is far enough below market to pick up the stock, but not so far below the current market price that the trade does not fill. You can calculate below-market limit orders as follows:

- If the Bull/Bear Rating is −5, which is extremely bearish, you can use a limit order of 50 percent of the EM below the most recent Friday closing price.
- If the Bull/Bear Rating is −4, you can use a limit order of 40 percent of the EM below the most recent Friday closing price.
- If the Bull/Bear Rating is −3, you can use a limit order of 30 percent of the EM below the most recent Friday closing price.
- If the Bull/Bear Rating is −2, you can use a limit order of 20 percent of the EM below the most recent Friday closing price.
- If the Bull/Bear Rating is −1, which is mildly bearish, you can use a limit order of 10 percent of the EM below the most recent Friday closing price.
- If the Bull/Bear Rating is 0, you can use a limit order of 5 percent of the EM below the most recent Friday closing price.
- If the Bull/Bear Rating is +1 to +4, which is bullish, you can use a limit order of 10 percent of the EM above the most recent Friday closing price.
- If the Bull/Bear Rating is +5, which is extremely bullish, you can use a limit order of 20 percent of the EM above the most recent Friday closing price.

Of course, when the Bull/Bear Rating is bullish to extremely bullish, you may have to pay up a bit to pick up your trade. Still, using the above calculations for your limit orders will help you buy on dips. This means your net cost of the trade, including broker sales commission, will likely be less than if you were buying at market.

Sector and Industry Charts

Now, let's move to the final set of charts that will help you time the market for opening a new position. Much of what I cover below, you learned in Rule 3, but here is where we tie everything together.

Keep in mind that to get to this point, you have made the following decisions:

1. You have found only the best stocks with the strongest Demand Fundamentals (Rule 1).
2. You have narrowed that list by comparing the relative price-to-earnings ratio (P/E) of each stock so that you are only looking at those stocks that are the best and cheapest in each peer group (Rule 2).
3. Of those stocks with exceptionally strong Demand Fundamentals, you have selected only those that are exhibiting a technical buy signal (Rule 3).
4. Based on the Historical Dow chart, you believe now is a good time to be putting money to work in the market (Rule 10).
5. Based on the Current Market Forecast, you believe now is an excellent time to be buying since it appears the market is poised to move higher in the near term (Rule 10).
6. Now, you want to make sure that the industry and sector are supporting the upward movement of your stock's pricing trend.

Figure 10.6 is a technical chart for AAPL: Apple Corporation.

(To refresh your memory: We discussed how to read this chart in Rule 3, "Trade like a Technician." The top portion of this Apple chart shows the trend line, technical buy signals, and, the technical short sell signals.)

As of this writing, this is a stock with very good Demand Fundamentals and excellent technicals, if you want to be long in a stock. Take a look at the industry (Personal Computers) and sector (technology) charts at the bottom of Figure 10.6.

The industry is Personal Computers. This chart represents the average price of every stock in the Personal Computer industry. This is the same type of chart that you learned about in Rule 3, but instead of it being a technical chart of a stock, it is a technical chart of an entire industry. This view of the market is extremely valuable, since you not only get to see what the stock is doing, but you get to see how the market is looking at the entire industry. Your stock is a part of that industry and a significant portion of the pricing trend of your stock is tied to the pricing trend of the entire industry. If the average price of every stock in the Personal Computer industry is moving higher (as in the case in Figure 10.6), then there is

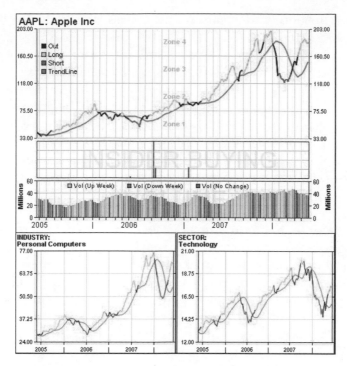

Figure 10.6   AAPL

upward pressure on your stock (in this case, AAPL) share price. Money is flowing into the Personal Computer industry. How do I know that? Just look at the far right side of the Personal Computer industry chart in Figure 10.6. Note how it has broken out strongly above its trend line. This is a very bullish indicator on the entire industry.

When the average price of all the stocks in an industry moves above the trend line, you should consider the industry in "bull mode." When the average price of all the stocks in an industry moves below the trend line, you should consider the industry in "bear mode."

It is a good thing to buy into industries that are in bull mode and sell into industries that are in bear mode.

The same logic used to determine bull mode and bear mode for industries can be used to determine bull mode and bear mode for sectors.

When investors are selling more shares than they are buying, it means demand is weakening and the price action will be lower. This is true for individual stocks, and for groups of stocks as in sectors and industries. It is important to watch the money flows. When investors start pumping money into an industry or a sector, nearly all of the stocks in those two categories will begin to have positive price action; meaning the market prices tend to move higher.

You will recall I said earlier "a rising tide lifts all boats and a lowering tide lowers all boats." The same thing happens here when it comes to watching the movement of sectors and industries. Let me explain:

1. When you buy a stock in an industry and sector where the average price of all the stocks is moving higher, it tends to put a positive push on your stock. Your stock, which will have its own reasons for moving higher or lower, will tend to have more upward pressure on its share price when the industry and sector are moving higher. Remember, almost 50 percent of a stock's price action is tied to its sector and industry.

2. When you buy a stock in an industry and sector where the average price of all the stocks is moving lower, it tends to put negative pressure on your stock's market price.

I like to buy stocks where everything possible is moving in my direction. I want the stock to have strong Demand Fundamentals; I want the stock's market price to be trending well above the trendline; I want the sector in bull mode; and I want the industry in bull mode.

When you sell a stock short, the opposite of everything I just told you is true:

- You want the stock to have weak Demand Fundamentals. Why? Strong Demand Fundamentals are a lot like mass. The bigger something is and the heavier it is, the harder it is to turn it. I like to use the example of trying to steer a large ocean liner in the water. It's much easier to steer a small fishing boat. When a stock with strong Demand Fundamentals is moving higher, those Demand Fundamentals tend to keep that stock moving higher. Likewise, a stock with weak Demand Fundamentals has little to push its market price higher. So, weak Demand

Fundamentals tend to be a good thing for shorting a stock and a bad thing for buying it long. In our AAPL example, the strong Demand Fundamentals are a negative for shorting the stock.

- You want the sector and industry (particularly, the industry) to be in bear mode. This means you want the week-ending closing prices for the sector and industry to be very red and moving lower. This tends to help push your stock's market price lower and lower, as more and more investors take money out of the sector and industry. This is the example of a lowering tide lowering all boats and helping push your short trade lower and lower.

What You Learned in This Rule

In this rule you learned how to make smart, timely decisions about when to get into a new stock and when to get out by watching the entire market. You learned:

- How to use broad market trends as leading indicators, to give you more insight and to properly position your stop loss settings to maximize your return while minimizing your downside risk.
- How to use a chart of the Dow 30 over the past century to determine broad market directional moves.
- How to use buy and short sell signals to forecast market corrections.
- How to use the ratio of bull signals to bear signals and the expected move of stocks to pick a smart way to set limit orders.
- How to use sectors and industry charts as potential negative or positive support for buying and short selling stocks.

Making the Commitment to Being a Rules-Based Investor

Thank you for spending a few hours with me. I hope you enjoyed reading and studying my 10 Essential Rules. I hope you have become more empowered to take control of your investments. I know from personal experience that your use of these rules will make you a wealthier, happier, and less stressed stock market investor.

Let's agree on one simple objective: You want to make consistent profits in the stock market, and I have given you the rules to make that happen. This book was written completely centered around and dedicated to that objective. I want this to now be your objective. I want you to notice I didn't say it is your "goal." Goals are great, but they often have a connotation of being just beyond our capabilities. Objectives, however, are definitely achievable.

For any objective worth achieving, there has to be a plan and a willingness to perform the necessary steps to attain the objective. My plan is for you to agree to follow my 10 Essential Rules by making a commitment to a disciplined course of action. Discipline is the absolute key to your success in this plan. You cannot follow 9 out of 10 of my rules and be consistently profitable. You cannot follow all 10 of these rules some of the time and not the rest of the time and be consistently profitable.

You have to commit to following all 10 rules all of the time—in good markets, bad markets, or trading-range markets.

You must be committed to letting these 10 rules govern the way you buy and sell stocks. You must be committed to replacing emotion with these 10 rules. Don't get me wrong; there will be plenty of opportunities for you to bring in an opinion based on current events, but not to the extent that your opinion violates the rules.

I want you to be a consistent winner in your stock investments. This, by the way, does *not* mean that every trade will make you a profit. To make consistent profits means that over time, you will make a greater number of profitable trades than losing trades. And, your losing trades will have consistently smaller losses. Plus, your winning trades will have consistently larger gains.

Remember, the key here is discipline. Don't give up and don't give in to your emotions. These rules work. They always work. You can absolutely bank on it.

Take advantage of the companion web site to the book: www.10EssentialRules.com. You will find more details and thousands of stocks that have been ranked and rated according to these rules. It will be a huge help to you as you get started putting these rules to work.

Make these 10 rules a part of your investment DNA and you will do well. Put them to work. You won't regret it!

Now, get out there and start making some serious money!

APPENDIX A

Understanding Stop Loss Orders

First, let's make sure you clearly understand just what a stop loss order is and what it is not:

There are three kinds of stop loss orders:

1. **Stop limit.** This is an order that says once the stock's market price touches or goes below the stop limit order price, the stop limit order is activated, but not necessarily filled. The broker is required to sell the stock at or above the stop limit order price, if and only if, there is a willing buyer who will pay the limit order price. Should the market price of the stock fall well below the stop limit order price (this is considered a "gap down"), then, although your stop limit order has been activated, it will not fill unless the market price of your stock rebounds back to or above your limit order price. Once the market price of your stock has plummeted below your limit order stop loss price, it could continue to move lower (even to zero) and your limit stop loss order will never fill. I do not recommend using stop limit orders.
2. **Stop market.** This type of stop loss order is known by various names, such as "stop," "stop loss," and "stop market." This is an order that says once the stock's market price touches or goes below the stop market order price, the stop market order is activated and filled as soon as there is a willing buyer (market), regardless of price. On the surface, this may sound very disconcerting. It is quite the contrary. If a stock is going to

trigger your stop loss price, even if it gaps below your stop loss price, you will want to get out of the stock as quickly as possible. I believe in the cockroach theory. The theory is that there is never only one cockroach. In the case of stocks, if a stock plummets below your stop loss setting, it is almost always because of some kind of bad news (the cockroach). And almost always, not all the bad news comes out at once. More bad news (more cockroaches) is likely to follow. Better to get out at any price than to hope the bad news will go away and the stock will rebound. Hope is a terrible investment strategy. I much prefer to use stop market stops over any other type of stop loss type of order.

3. **Trailing stop.** Trailing stops are designed to follow the market price of a stock by a percentage amount or fixed dollar amount. The higher the market price of the stock, the higher will move the trailing stop. If the stock's market price moves lower, the trailing stop will not move. The concept is that you can merely set the maximum amount that a stock can move lower to trigger the stop. Once the market price of the stock touches or falls below the trailing stop price, the stock is then sold at market to the next willing buyer. I rarely use trailing stops. They are virtually guaranteed to take you out of a position. Each little uptick in a stock's price will pull the stop loss order higher and higher, eventually triggering the stop on the next downward tick of the stock's market price. Here is an example of why I don't like trailing stops:

Let's say that you own a stock that was trading at $40 per share when the market opened on Monday and you had a $4 trailing stop. At the following Friday close, the stock was trading at $60 per share.

Of course, you would expect your stop not to have triggered and that now it is sitting at $56.

What you don't know is that you stopped out at $38 per share. Here is how it happened:

- The stock moved to $42 per share. When it did, the trailing stop moved to $38 per share.

- Then, the stock moved to $38 per share and you stopped out.
- Then, the stock moved back up to $40, then $45, then $50 and then finally at $60 per share.

If you had used a stop market of $36 per share, your stop would not have triggered because the stock never traded at or below $36. It is important that you give a stock enough room for normal volatility. Placing your stops too close to the market price (i.e., well within the expected move) is just asking for a stop out. This is why I generally adjust my stops only once a week.

Regardless of the type of stop loss order, you are *not* guaranteed that you will get your price. All a stop loss order does is provide a "trigger price," such that when the market price of a stock falls to or below that trigger price, a trade is activated, but not necessarily filled.

B

Scoring the Fundamentals

When it comes to deciding which stocks to buy, you have learned that 50 percent of your decision must be based on the stock's fundamentals. In Rule 1, you learned that there are a few fundamentals that matter the most when selecting stocks. These are called Demand Fundamentals, and are listed below:

- Quarter-over-quarter revenue growth rate
- Year-over-year earnings growth rate
- Quarter-over-quarter earnings growth rate
- Five-year average revenue growth rate
- Five-year average earnings growth rate
- Return on equity
- Dividend yield

Investors tend to have a significant reaction to changes in these fundamentals. The better the numbers, the more investors will drive up demand for shares and, consequently, the higher the price for shares becomes. Therefore, when selecting stocks to buy, the stronger these Demand Fundamentals, the better. Remember, your goal is to own stocks that have the highest likelihood of increasing share price.

In Rule 2, you learned of an additional key fundamental that is based on relative value, where you compare a stock's PE to its peer group or industry.

Certainly, it is a straightforward process to compare all stocks in your universe by these Demand Fundamentals. All you have to do is calculate the rates of growth (or find one of the many free services online that calculate these rates for you) for each stock and compare the results of one stock to another.

The task of finding these Demand Fundamentals is not hard, but it does become a bit daunting to have seven different values for each stock and attempt to find the best stock by comparing these seven values from stock to stock.

I have developed a simple way to quickly find the stock with the best Demand Fundamentals and it is something you can easily do on your own.

The first thing you will want to do is to assign a numeric score to each Demand Fundamental. I score each one from a low of zero to a high of nine. Then, all you have to do is add up the scores for each stock's Demand Fundamentals to get a total score. The stock with the highest score has the best Demand Fundamentals. The stock with the lowest score has the worst.

Below is a suggested scoring template to use for each of the Demand Fundamentals. Following this section is a simple Excel worksheet that shows you how easy it is to rate and rank dozens of stocks with regard to this important fundamental analysis.

Scoring the Fundamentals

- **Quarter-over-quarter revenue growth rate.** Scoring quarter-over-quarter revenue growth rates requires that you first calculate the rate of growth from the year ago quarter results for revenue to the most recent quarter results for revenue. Then, assign a score to those results. To calculate the rate of revenue growth, measure how much a stock's total revenue increased or decreased from the amount of revenue generated by the company in the year-ago quarter to the most recent quarter. For example, let's assume Company XYZ had quarterly revenue in the year-ago quarter of 10 percent. In the most recently reported quarter, the company reported revenue of 10.2 percent. The rate of growth would be (10.2 percent − 10 percent)/10 percent × 100 = 2 percent.

One you have the rate of growth between the year ago quarter and the most recent quarter, for total revenue, your next step is to assign a score for the results. Following is a recommended scoring structure for this Demand Fundamental:

- 12 for rates greater than or equal to 30 percent.
- 8 for rates greater than or equal to 15 percent and less than 30 percent.
- 6 for rates greater than or equal to 5 percent and less than 15 percent.
- 4 for rates greater than or equal to 0 percent and less than 5 percent.
- 2 for rates greater than or equal to −5 percent and less than 0 percent.
- 0 for rates less than −5 percent.

- **Year-over-year earnings growth rate:** Compare the total earnings for the previous year to the total earnings for the most recent year and then determine the percentage increase or decrease. For example, let's assume Company XYZ had annual earnings last year of 14 percent. In the most recently reported year, the company reported earnings of 8 percent. The rate of growth would be (8 percent − 14 percent)/ 14 percent × 100 = −42 percent. The growth rate of this company went down by 42 percent!

  The scoring for this Demand Fundamental is:

  - 12 for rates greater than 50 percent.
  - 8 for rates greater than 15 percent and less than 50 percent.
  - 6 for rates greater than 5 percent and less than 15 percent.
  - 4 for rates greater than 0 percent and less than 5 percent.
  - 2 for rates greater than −5 percent and less than 0 percent.
  - 0 for rates less than −5 percent.

- **Quarter-over-quarter earnings growth rate.** Compare the total earnings for the quarter, one year ago, to the total earnings for the most recent quarter and then determine the percentage increase or decrease. For example, let's assume Company XYZ had quarterly earnings in the year-ago quarter of 5 percent. In the most recently reported quarter, the company reported earnings of 10 percent. The rate of growth would be (10 percent − 5 percent)/5 percent × 100 = 100 percent. Earnings growth of 100 percent is huge, and investors will pay up for these shares.

The scoring for this Demand Fundamental is:

- 12 for rates greater than 50 percent.
- 8 for rates greater than 15 percent and less than 50 percent.
- 6 for rates greater than 5 percent and less than 15 percent.
- 4 for rates greater than 0 percent and less than 5 percent.
- 2 for rates greater than −5 percent and less than 0 percent.
- 0 for rates less than −5 percent.

- **Five-year average earnings growth rate.** Go back six years and calculate the rate of growth of earnings from year 5 to year 4, then from year 4 to year 3, and so on, until you have the yearly earnings growth rate for each year. Then add these five rates together and divide by five for the five-year average earnings growth rate. For example, let's assume Company XYZ had the following annual earnings growth rates for the previous five years: 2 percent, 5 percent, 3 percent, 8 percent and 9 percent. The average annual earnings growth rate would be (2 percent + 5 percent + 3 percent + 8 percent + 9 percent) ÷ 5 = 5.4 percent.

The scoring for this Demand Fundamental is:

- 12 for rates greater than 20 percent.
- 8 for rates greater than 10 percent and less than 20 percent.
- 6 for rates greater than 5 percent and less than 10 percent.
- 4 for rates greater than 0 percent and less than 5 percent.
- 2 for rates greater than −5 percent and less than 0 percent.
- 0 for rates less than −5 percent.

- **Five-year average revenue growth rate.** Go back six years and calculate the rate of growth of revenue from year 5 to year 4, then from year 4 to year 3, and so on, until you have the yearly Revenue Growth rate for each year. Then add these five rates together and divide by five for the 5-year average revenue growth rate. For example, let's assume Company XYZ had the following annual revenue growth rates for the previous five years: 12 percent, 5 percent, 30 percent, 10 percent and 12 percent. The average annual earnings growth rate would be (12 percent + 5 percent + 30 percent + 10 percent + 12 percent) ÷ 5 = 7.8 percent.

The scoring for this Demand Fundamental is:

- 12 for growth rates greater than 50 percent.
- 8 for growth rates greater than or equal to 20 percent and less than 50 percent.

- 6 for growth rates greater than or equal to 5 percent and less than 20 percent.
- 4 for growth rates greater than or equal to 0 percent and less than 5 percent.
- 2 for growth rates greater than or equal to −5 percent and less than 0 percent.
- 0 for growth rates less than −5 percent.
- **Return on equity.** Return on equity is the return generated by the company for each dollar of shareholder investment. This is a way to determine how effectively the shareholder's investment is being employed by the company. This value needs to be 15 percent or higher; the higher the better. Return on equity is calculated by dividing the annual earnings by common shareholders equity, which is equal to total assets minus total liabilities.

  The scoring for this Demand Fundamental is:
- 10 for rates greater than 20 percent.
- 8 for rates greater than 15 percent and less than 20 percent.
- 6 for rates greater than 10 percent and less than 15 percent.
- 4 for rates greater than 5 percent and less than 10 percent.
- 2 for rates greater than 0 percent and less than 5 percent.
- 0 for rates less than 0 percent.
- **Dividend yield.** Stocks with high-paying dividends are not always the best stocks to own for significant growth in share price. But in those rare instances where a stock's other Demand Fundamentals are strong *and* that stock happens to have a strong dividend, you can certainly consider that a big plus. Most investors prefer higher-yielding stocks and when a company increases its dividend, it generally gets a nice bump up in share price. Therefore, dividend yield is another one of the Demand Fundamentals, which is scored as following:
- 10 for yields equal to or greater than 5 percent.
- 4 for yields greater than 0 percent and less than 5 percent.
- 0 for yields less than or equal to 0.
- **PE.** It is always important to pay the least amount for the best stocks. This is another way to say you want to buy the stocks with the most value. Value is measured in terms of earnings and the amount of dollars it takes to buy those earnings. PE is nothing more than the price of a stock divided by its most

recent earnings per share. This is a very good way of comparing one stock's value (PE) to another.

But, as you learned in Rule 2, the only time that this comparison should be done is when comparing a stock's PE to another stock in its peer (or industry) group.

You can know how expensive or cheap (from a value perspective) a stock is by comparing its PE to the average PE of its industry. If the stock's PE is much higher than the average PE of the Industry, it is considered over valued. If its PE is much lower than the average PE of the industry, it is considered undervalued.

Following is a suggested methodology for scoring each stock's PE (the higher the score the more value in the stock):

- 0 for a PE that is more than 50 percent greater than the Industry's average PE.
- 4 for a PE that is greater than or equal to the industry's average PE but not more than 50 percent above the industry's average PE.
- 6 for a PE that is less than the industry's average PE but not less than 50 percent below the industry's average PE.
- 10 for a PE that is less than 50 percent below the industry's average PE by 50 percent.

- **Institutional ownership.** One does not normally think of institutional ownership as a fundamental, but for 99 percent of investors, it should be. In fact, it should be considered a fundamental for any investor other than an institutional investor. You learned in Rule 7 that we, as individual investors, can make certain assumptions about the strength and quality of a company by how much of the outstanding shares are owned by institutions.

  You learned that if institutions own too much of the outstanding shares, it increases your risk of a major and rapid sell-off. You also learned that if a company has no institutional ownership, it means that the big institutions have reviewed the company's potential to generate increasing share price, and have passed. In other words, a company with no institutional ownership is considered fundamentally weak.

  So, it is a good idea to rate and score institutional ownership, as follows:

  - 10 for institutional ownership between 30 percent and 60 percent.

- 7 for institutional ownership between 10 percent and 30 percent, and between 60 percent and 90 percent.
- 5 for institutional ownership greater than 1 percent but less than 10 percent, and for institutional ownership below 98 percent and 90 percent.
- 0 for institutional ownership that equals 0 or for institutional ownership greater than 98 percent.

About the Author

Mike Turner is the founder of TurnerTrends, an online subscription-based advisory service, which provides his clients with the investor tools for planning their investment strategies. Many of his clients are building and managing their own world-class portfolios using the stock analysis software tools he has developed. His newsletter is gaining in popularity because of his unique stock-selling methodology, which he has patented, called the Intelligent Stop Loss®. He also has patents pending on other aspects of his portfolio analysis system.

Mr. Turner is also the founder and president of Sabinal Capital Investments, LLC, which is a registered investment advisory. It is through Sabinal that Mike and his staff manage money for higher net worth clients.

He is a much-sought-after speaker at investment trading venues around the country, including the World Money Show, Trader's Expo, and American Association of Individual Investors (AAII) meetings. His advice on stock selection, stock selling, exchange-traded funds (ETFs), and his 10 Essential Rules are his most popular topics.

Mr. Turner graduated from Oklahoma State University, with a degree in civil engineering. It is his analytical background, extensive computer skills, and commonsense approach to the stock market that allowed him to develop the powerful software system that analyzes over 6,000 stocks every week. This program sifts through the data to help him find and select good stocks to buy, and also tells him when it is time to sell. This information has allowed his clients the opportunity to realize their financial dreams in bull markets and bear markets.

Prior to his involvement in the stock market, Mr. Turner was the founder, developer, and president of a company that wrote enterprise-level software systems that were used by medical research facilities and pharmaceutical companies worldwide. His clients included nearly all of the world's major pharmaceutical companies and medical research facilities that were doing preclinical drug safety studies. He was there until he sold his company in 1997.

Mr. Turner is currently the editor of his weekly online newsletter and serves as the portfolio manager of each of the TurnerTrends portfolios (www.turnertrends.com). More information about Sabinal Capital Investments can be obtained through www.sabinalcapital.com.

Index

A
Accumulation/distribution
    index, 55
Analysis
  of company, 16
  fundamental, 21, 25
  technical, 53–54
Annualized return, calculating, 70
Appel, Gerald, 56
Average true range, 56
Averaging down, 9. *See also*
    Doubling down

B
Bankruptcy laws, 18
Baruch, Bernard, 77
Basic materials sector, industries
    in, 127
Basis investment, of portfolios,
    139
  original, 139
Bear markets, 14, 65, 169–70
Below-market limit orders, 167
Beta, 24
Bias, short, 161
Bogle, John, 7
Bollinger, John, 56
Bollinger bands, 56, 66
Breakout, 56
Buffett, Warren, 16, 40, 41, 112
Bull markets, 14, 65, 169–70

Buy-and-hold strategy, 12
Buying
  insider, 106–8
  reasons for, 79
  timing of, 156
  "what you know," 95

C
Capital goods sector, industries in,
    127–28
Cash, in investment, 150–51
Change, rate of, 31
Charts
  building technical, 60–67
  Dow, 159
  industry, 64–65, 159, 168–71
  point and figure, 57
  price activity (PAC), 56–57
  reading, 57–60
  sector, 65, 159, 168–71
  technical, 68–70
Closing bell, 87
Comfort zone, investment, 4
Company
  analysis of, 16
  equity portion of, 24
  financials, 20–21
  performance of, 25
  products of, 98–99
  research on, 99–100
  value of, 40

Consolidation period, 160
Consumer cyclical sector,
    industries in, 128
Consumer goods sector,
    industries in, 128–29
Consumer non-cyclical sector,
    industries in, 129
Corporate earnings,
    increasing, 47
Correction forecast, 162–65
Current value
    of portfolio, 146, 151
    of stock, 141

D
Dahl theory, 56
Day traders, 156
Decision making, technical
    analysis and, 67–68
Demand. *See* Supply and
    demand
Demand fundamentals, 24, 29,
    30–34, 38, 46, 48, 168
    comparing, 39
    scoring example, 34
    spreadsheet example, 33
Derivative, 18
Distribution
    determining industry,
        141–42
    determining sector, 142–44
    percentage, 146
Diversification, 121–46
    definition of, 124
    enforcing, 136–40
    industries and, 127–36
    by industry, 141–42
    reason for, 121–24
    by sector, 142–44
    strategy, 124–36, 145–46
Dividends, 98
Dividend yield, 30, 33, 183

Doubling down, 9. *See also*
    Averaging down
Dow, 14
    Historical Dow chart, 159
Downside risk, 80

E
Earnings
    corporate, 47
    growth rate of, 39
Earnings per share (EPS), 47
Efficient market hypothesis
    (EMH), xv
Elliot Wave theory, xv
Emotional trading, 96
Emotions
    avoiding loving stocks, 101–2
    investing and, 7–10
    removing from investing,
        10–12, 93–102
Excel spreadsheet, demand
    fundamentals and, 33
Exchange-traded funds (ETF), 85,
    150, 151
Expected move (EM), 86, 166
Exponential moving average
    (EMA), 56

F
Fibonacci analysis, xv
Financial reports, 25
Financial sector, industries in,
    130–31
Five-year average earnings growth
    rate, 30, 33, 182
Five-year average revenue growth
    rate, 182–83
Flow, stop loss rule and, 73–76
Fundamental analysis, 21, 25
Fundamental investors, 21
Fundamentalist, definition
    of, 20

Fundamentalist thinking, investing and, 15–36
Fundamentals
  demand, 24, 29, 30–34
  general, 22
  risk and, 23–26
  scoring, 179–85
Funds
  exchange-traded, 85, 150, 151
  mutual, 14

G
Gains, unrealized, 72, 77
General fundamentals, 22
Goal achievement, 27–28
Google, Inc., trading action on, 89–90
Growth, negative, 31
Growth rate, 39
  definition of, 31
  five-year average earnings, 30, 32, 182
  five-year average revenue, 182–83
  quarter-over-quarter earnings, 30, 32, 181–83
  quarter-over-quarter revenue, 30, 32, 180–81
  year-over-year earnings, 30, 32, 181

H
Health care sector, industries in, 131
Herd mentality, in investing, 74
Hikkake pattern, 56
Historical Dow chart, 159
Historical volatility (HV), 86
Hunch trading, 11
Hutson, Jack, 57

I
Indexes, 6–7
  accumulation/distribution, 55
  relative strength, 57
  S&P 500 index fund, 7, 14, 45, 47, 160
Industrial goods sector, industries in, 132
Industries
  in basic materials sector, 127
  in capital goods sector, 127–28
  in consumer cyclical sector, 128
  in consumer goods sector, 128–29
  in consumer non-cyclical sector, 129
  in financial sector, 130–31
  in health care sector, 131
  in industrial goods sector, 132
  in services sector, 132–34
  in technology sector, 134–35
  in transportation sector, 135–36
  in utilities sector, 136
Industry, 125
  charts, 64–65, 159, 168–71
  determining distribution, 141–42
Inflation, stock market and, 6
Insider buying, 64
Insider selling, 105
Insider trading, 103–8
  definition of, 104
  legal side of, 105–6
  using insider buying information, 106–8
Institutional ownership, 109–19, 184–85
  charting, 114–17
  definition of, 113
  downside to, 118
  interpreting, 117–19
  rules of thumb, 118–19

Institutional trading, using,
   113–14
Intelligent Stop Loss rule, 60, 66,
   71, 83–85, 93
Intuition, investing and, 11
Investment
   basis, 139
   bridging 10 rules, 50–51
   cash in, 150–51
   comfort zone, 4
   emotions and, 7–10
   fundamentalist thinking and,
      15–36
   habits, 12–14
   intuition and, 11
   long-term horizon, 157–59
   methodology, 28
   reasons for, 2–3
   removing emotions from,
      10–12
   timing of, 23
Investment DNA, 80
Investors
   fundamental, 21
   momentum, 157
   rules-based, 173–74
   value, 40

J
Jobs, Steve, 97

L
Lagging indicators, 25
Law of diminishing returns, 16
Long position, 62
Long-term investment horizon,
   157–59
Loss, unrealized, 72, 77
Loss comfort zone, 84
Losses, in stock market, 4–5
   profits *versus*, 5

Love, for stocks, 101–2
Lynch, Peter, 95

M
Market Bias Fund, xvii
Market cap, 18, 19
Market correction, 163, 164
Markets
   bear, 14, 65
   bull, 14, 65
   definition of, 158
Market timer, 157
Market trend, 162–65
Market Trend portfolio, xvi
Mohindar, Rahul, 57
Momentum and rate of
   change, 56
Momentum investor, 157
Money flow in technical
   analysis, 56
Moves against you, 81
Moving average convergence/
   divergence (MACD), 56
Mutual funds, 6–7, 14
   underperformance of, 6

N
Nasdaq, 14
Neff, John, 40
Negative growth, 31

O
On-balance volume, 56
Options traders, 156
Original basis investment, 139
Outlier, 69
Overweighted, 117

P
Parabolic stop and reverse
   (SAR), 57
Percentage distribution, 146

Pivot point, 57
Point and figure charts, 57
Portfolios
    asset allocation by stock, 152
    basis investment of, 139
    building, 38
    current value of, 146, 151
    diversification of, 105,
        121–24, 137
    equally weighted, 149–53
    example of, 138, 140, 143
    Market Trend, xvi
    running totals in, 72
    size of, 48–49
    10 Must Follow Rules portfolio,
        xvii
    time management of, 151
Price, Michael, 40
Price activity (PAC) charts, 56–57
Price line, 59–60
Prices
    avoiding high, with PE ratio,
        43–45
    moves against you and, 81
Price-to-back (PB) ratio, 40
Price-to-earnings (PE) ratio, 39,
        40, 42, 71, 183–84
    avoiding high price with,
        43–45
    avoiding misconception, 45–48
    reasonable ranges, 44
    stock selection and, 50
Pricing trends, use of, 53–70
Profits
    failure to make consistent, 4–6
    losses *versus*, 5
    making in stock market, 1
    risk and, 148–49

Q
Quarter-over-quarter earnings
    growth rate, 30, 32, 181–82

Quarter-over-quarter revenue
    growth rate, 30, 32, 180–81

R
Rahul Mohindar oscillator
    (RMO), 57
Rate of change, 31
Rate of growth, 31
Real estate investment trusts
    (REIT), 123
Relative strength index, 57
Reports
    10-K, 25, 26
    10-Q, 25, 26
Research, on company, 17,
    99–100
Return on equity, 30, 33, 183
Risk
    acceptable level of, 79
    definition of, 23
    downside, 80
    fundamentals and, 23–26
    stop loss rule and, 74
Risk assessment rule, 147–54
    equally weighted portfolios
        and, 149–53
    minimizing risk, 148–49
Rules-based investor, becoming,
    173–74

S
Sabinal Capital Investments,
    LLC, xvii
Scoring fundamentals, 179–85
Sector, 125
    charts, 65, 159, 168–71
    determining distribution,
        142–44
Securities and Exchange
    Commission (SEC), 26, 104
Selling stocks, 78–80
    timing of, 156

Services sector, industries in, 132–34
Shareholders, rights as, 17–19
Shareholder value, 24
Shares
  demand for, 29
  owning in company, 100
Short bias, 161
Short position, 63
Sideways, 75
S&P 500 index fund, 7, 14, 45, 47, 160
Splits, 63
Standard deviation, 86
Stewart, Martha, 104
Stochastic oscillator, 57
Stock collecting, 12
Stock market
  failure to make consistent profits in, 4–6
  making profits in, 1
  reasons for investing in, 2–3
Stocks
  under accumulation, 116
  avoid loving, 101–2
  buying strategies, 48–49
  current value of, 141
  under distribution, 116
  infatuation with, 94–96
  marriage to, 98–101
  primary reason to own, 76–78
  reason for buying, 79
  selling, 78–80
Stock selection, 15–36
  demand fundamentals and, 29, 30–34
  fundamentalist thinking and, 20–23
  goal achievement and, 27–28
  objective, 19–20
  PE ratio and, 50

PE reasonable ranges and, 44
reduction of choices, 35–36
risk and, 23–26
shareholder rights, 17–19
supply and demand and, 28–29
Stock selection refinement rule, 109–19
  charting institutional ownership, 114–17
  interpreting institutional ownership, 117–19
  misleading personalities and experts, 110–11
  problems with major institutions, 111–12
  using institutional trading, 113–14
  Wall Street titans and, 112–13
Stop limit, 175
Stop loss orders, 84
  understanding, 175–77
Stop loss price, volatility and, 85–90
Stop loss rule, 71–91, 97
  flow and, 73–76
  Intelligent Stop Loss strategy and, 83–85
  primary reason to own stocks, 76–78
  risk and, 74
  selling stocks, 78–80
  timing and, 80–83
  volatility and stop loss price and, 85–90
Stop loss strategy, 66
Stop market, 175
Street expectations, 25
Supply and demand, 28–29
  curve, 29
Swing traders, 157

T
Technical analysis, 53–54
  building charts, 60–67
  decision making and, 67–68
  methodology, 55
  money flow in, 56
  perspective and, 54–55
  reading charts, 57–60, 68–70
  systems, 55–57
Technical charts
  building, 60–67
  reading, 68–70
Technology sector, industries in,
    134–35
Television personalities,
    recommendations from,
    110–11
Templeton, John, 40
10-K reports, 25, 26
10 Must follow rules
  bridge between, 50–51
  diversification rule, 121–46
  insider trading rule, 103–8
  removing emotion rule, 93–102
  risk assessment rule, 147–54
  stock selection, 15–36
  stock selection refinement rule,
    109–19
  stop loss rule, 71–91
  technical analysis rule, 53–70
  timing rule, 155–71
  value rule, 37–51
10 Must Follow Rules portfolio, xvii
10-Q reports, 25, 26
Ten-week moving average trend
    line, 58–59
Timing
  definition of, 158
  Historical Dow chart and,
    159–62
  of investment, 23

market trend and correction
    forecast, 162–65
  rule, 155–71
  stop loss rule and, 80–83
Tipping, of information, 104
Total Market Forecast, 159
Traders
  day, 156
  options, 156
  swing, 157
Trading
  emotional, 96
  for free, 165–67
  fundamentalist thinking
    and, 15
  insider, 103–8
  institutional, 113–14
  rules, set of, 5
  sideways, 75
  volume, 108
Trading action on Google, Inc.,
    89–90
Trailing stop, 176
Transportation sector, industries
    in, 135–36
Trend line, 59, 88
  10-week moving average,
    58–59
Trix oscillator, 57
TurnerTrends, Inc., xvi

U
Under accumulation, 116
Under distribution, 116
Unrealized gains, 72, 77
Unrealized loss, 72, 77
Utilities sector, industries in, 136

V
Value
  investor, 40
  shareholder, 24

Value rule, 37–51
  avoiding PE misconception, 45–48
  as incorrect strategy, 40–43
  PE ratios and stock price, 43–45
  portfolio size and, 48–49
Vetted, 110
Volatility, 23, 24, 84
  historical, 86
  stop loss price and, 85–90
Volume
  on-balance, 56
  trading, 108
  weekly trading, 64

W
Waksal, Sam, 104, 105
Wall Street titans, 112–13
Weekly Bull/Bear Forecast, 159
Weekly trading volume, 64
Whipsaw, 71
Wilder, J. Welles, 56, 57
Williams, Larry, 57
Williams %R oscillator, 57

Y
Year-over-year earnings growth rate, 30, 32, 181

Z
Zones, 63–64
  loss comfort, 84